AN IRON-WILLED GIANT

The story of Clarence LeBus and the small Kentucky tobacco farmers that he led in their struggle with the American Tobacco Company.

MARK MATTMILLER

An Iron-Willed Giant
Copyright © 2021

by Mark Mattmiller

No part of this book may be reproduced in any manner whatsoever without written permission except in the case of brief quotations embodied in critical articles and reviews.

All Rights Reserved. Printed in the United States of America.

For information, address Cloud 9 Press,
634 Central Ave, Lexington, KY 40502.
ISBN: 978-0-9894367-8- 6

Cover and Illustrations, Interior Design
by Chip Holtzhauer

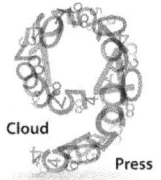

Cloud
Press

Thanks To:

Jack DuArte

Bill Thompson

Erin Mattmiller

Introduction

The small town of Cynthiana, Kentucky has two living heroes of which we, as citizens, are all proud. Surely everyone living here knows that the former coach of the University of Kentucky basketball team, Joe B. Hall, was born and raised in our town. Equally renowned is our local citizen, Robert Kirkman, who is the creator of *The Walking Dead*.

While there is nobody living today who remembers Clarence LeBus or the tobacco wars, a large part of the community is still aware of the history of the conflict and of the life of Mr. LeBus himself. Certainly in the late eighteenth and early nineteenth centuries he was "The Man."

Even today, but only occasionally, a story will be told, an old photograph presented, or a crumbling newspaper clipping presented that again brings the name of Clarence LeBus to the forefront. I'm sure that I hear and witness a little more of this sort of thing than the average resident, because my wife, Linda, is the great-granddaughter of Clarence LeBus.

Over the years, I have developed an interest in the man and an urge to tell the story of his life. Thus the book you now have before you: a story of the life of Clarence Lebus, the epic struggles of the Kentucky burley tobacco farmers facing the brutal monopolies of the American Tobacco Company, and LeBus's role in that fervid conflict.

Chapter One

Tobacco production in central Kentucky has always been the backbone of the area's agricultural endeavors. Early on, the composite social and the economic essence of every community was defined by the tobacco crop. Beginning with the first settlers in the 1700's, the planting, harvesting and selling of the crop were the most important features of farm-family life.

The families tilling the small hill farms depended on the cash from selling the crop to buy the things that they were unable to produce themselves. It didn't take much. Selling the tobacco was never a problem until about 1900 when James Duke and his American Tobacco Company managed to monopolize and control almost all cigarette production. It was then that Duke cut the prices paid for the crops to less than the cost of production.

The farmers reacted with the formation of an organization designed to hold the crop off the market and force Duke to pay more. Clarence LeBus led the farmers in their epic holdout struggle. The strife was to become known as The Kentucky Tobacco Wars.

Certainly the place of Clarence LeBus in the archives of history rests on his leadership in the burley tobacco union, but his success was in no way limited to that. His agricultural, banking, and business success was astounding.

A glimpse into his life can be seen in a newspaper article published six months after his death. The piece recounted a Christmas party held by his widow and two sons in his honor inside one of their tobacco warehouses.

From The Cynthiana Democrat, December 27, 1928:

> The largest private Christmas entertainment event ever held in Cynthiana and possibly the largest in Kentucky was that of Mrs. Clarence LeBus Sr., Mr. and Mrs. Frazer LeBus, and Mr. and Mrs. Clarence LeBus Jr., when they entertained the more than three hundred employees and tenants of the Clarence LeBus Estate Monday afternoon at 4 o'clock in the new tobacco warehouse of Clarence LeBus and Sons Company on Church Street. A crowd estimated at more than six hundred attended.
>
> A giant Christmas tree, strikingly decorated and brilliantly lighted was placed in the center of the warehouse floor. Surrounding it at the base were hundreds of toys and tobacco baskets filled with fruits, and hanging from beams were dozens of stalks of bananas. Tied to the poles and beams were hundreds of bright colored toy balloons. For family gifts, baskets containing turkeys, chickens, flour, sugar and groceries were provided. These were given to holders of tickets. In the corner of the warehouse was a free lunch stand, serving frankfurters, coffee, doughnuts, and ice cream cones. The affair was the most bountifully supplied that has been seen here.
>
> More of a gala appearance was given the warehouse by festooning posts with brightly-hued paper ropes and streamers. During the afternoon, old time melodies by a fiddle and three guitar players and a Negro servant of the LeBus's tripling on a harmonica, accordion and Jew's harp, enlivened the entertainment.
>
> John Cummins, tobacco auctioneer, in the role of Santa Claus, mingled with the crowd, shaking hands

with the children before taking his place in the circle reserved for the Christmas tree and distributing the gifts. For two hours the gifts were passed out, and after everyone had been supplied with more than they had anticipated, there was still a goodly quantity left. Assisting Santa Claus were Mrs. LeBus Sr., Mrs. Clarence LeBus Jr., Mrs. Frazer Lebus, Mrs. Clarence Ewing, and Mrs. J. W. Switzer. Messrs. LeBus with employees of the warehouse passed through the crowd with baskets of fruit and balloons.

The Clarence LeBus estate is possibly the largest in Kentucky history and has the greatest number of tenants. It is interesting to note that many of the veterans of the estate are proud of the length of their service. John Arnold started as a tenant thirty-two years ago and for the past ten years has been on one of the most valuable farms, the Claude Desha place. I.T.Whalen has spent twenty-nine years as tenant on the LeBus farms and E.T.Ashcraft more than sixteen years. Many have been with the LeBuses ten years or more. Richard Petticord has been an employee for thirty years.

While the attendance at the entertainment Monday afternoon was very large, many of the tenants from Bracken, Pendleton and Henry counties failed to arrive, and it is said that the full roster would have taxed the capacity of the warehouse. Whether belonging to the estate or not, no one present at the entertainment failed to receive some sort of present. It is estimated that the entertainment cost $2000.[1] (Sic)

Three hundred employees in hill country, and twenty nine thousand dollars (at today's value) for a Christmas party in small-town Cynthiana are both hard to imagine.

The inner Bluegrass Region of Kentucky is well known for its beautiful farms and fields. The gently rolling meadows are of the most productive black loam soil; the farms are large; and their owners quite prosperous.

A distinct change in the features cannot be missed when one travels north out of central Kentucky. The flat land gives way to hilly terrain and the loam soil becomes primarily red clay. This outer Bluegrass Region is unique in its geography and is the home of Harrison County and Cynthiana, Kentucky.

A culture of close-knit neighbors sharing work and equipment was established when the community was first settled. The county consisted mostly of small, poor hill-farms where most of the owners were farming for subsistence. There were nice, flat, and productive ridge-lands that gave way to draws and hollows on each side. The sloping hillsides were used for pasture and hay fields; usually the steepest were wooded. Sometimes there were narrow bottoms along the creeks and branches at the foot of a hill. Most every farmer had just enough flat ridge-land or small creek bottoms to raise an acre or two of tobacco for a cash crop. The labor requirements for raising tobacco were considerable, and neighbor helping neighbor was the norm.

There was not much going on in Cynthiana, Kentucky in late 1800s and the early 1900s. The town of only 7,000 people was, and is still, the county seat of Harrison County, Kentucky. There was no industry as we know it today in tiny Cynthiana. Automobiles were new to the scene. Telephones were a rare luxury, and prohibition was the cause of the day. Neither electricity nor running water had reached beyond the city limits. The commerce of the town was geared solely towards serving the farm families. Neighboring Bracken, Pendleton, and Henry counties were just as hilly and marginal as Harrison County. Small family farms, one-man businesses, and a slow pace were the elements of the day.

Clarence LeBus lived and farmed in this environment from 1862 until 1928. *The Cynthiana Log Cabin* (the town's second newspaper) reported Mr. LeBus's death in their June 26, 1928 issue. The article covered the entire front page. Clarence LeBus obviously accomplished a lot, but one astonishing fact stood out: He owned over 37,000 acres in six different counties at the time of his death.[2]

Chapter Two

It was not unusual for Clarence LeBus to tell the story of his having picked gooseberries for Betsy Hobson when he was eight years old. Mrs. Hobson was a neighboring lady, and young Clarence's pay was one half of the proceeds from the sale of the berries. While he didn't exactly say it, the message of his story was that he had a tough beginning growing up in a family that struggled financially. This was just not the case. Clarence's father, Lewis LeBus, was in fact exceedingly successful in farming and business. Lewis LeBus was never poor; he was thrifty. He saved every penny that he possibly could from what he earned. His intent was to eventually invest his savings in farmland, and that is exactly what he did. Lewis LeBus's son, Clarence, was never indulged, but he was, without doubt, surrounded by evidence of success.[1]

Lewis LeBus was born in 1834. He was the fifth child of Seraphin LeBus who had emigrated from Alsace, France/Germany to Lisbon, Ohio in 1828. Seraphin was of German heritage. Lewis LeBus was first educated in the local district schools, and then at age seventeen he was sent to the classical school at Salem, Ohio. After one year at Salem, he returned to his home county and taught there at the local common school. At the end of the third year of his teaching in Ohio he heard of greater opportunity in the south, moved to Oddville, Harrison County, Kentucky in the summer of 1855, and took a job teaching in the local one room school. Oddville was a tiny community six miles northeast of the town of Cynthiana. Lewis Lebus was twenty-one years old when he moved to Kentucky.

By 1860, through the application of the most ridged economy, and by working during his vacations in the fields, Lewis LeBus, Clarence's father, had saved enough to buy a small farm. It was during this same year that Lewis married Martha Garnett of Harrison County. Two sons followed in quick succession: first Orie in 1862 and then Clarence LeBus in 1863. Ultimately Lewis and Martha had seven children. They were: Orie, Clarence, Fanny, Leona, Bertha, Prentice, and Elizabeth.[2]

Lewis Lebus's fortunes grew quickly. He bought a second farm, and the income and savings from the two provided him with enough to buy a third. Lewis's farming enterprises continued to grow rapidly. Raising and selling tobacco provided a large part of the capital that fueled his dramatic growth. He believed that farmland should be bought to keep, not to be sold later. His attitude of frugality, his lifetime habit of never backing down from hard work, and his drive to improve himself financially were the substance of the man.[3]

The two oldest sons were introduced to the tobacco business at an early age. They both worked in the fields and the stripping rooms from early childhood until adulthood. Except for a short stint in college, Clarence was always employed one way or the other in the tobacco arena. He made a local reputation as an expert in the tobacco business, and it was early in his career that his reputation spread to the large tobacco centers in the United States. His services were soon sought as a buyer by the big tobacco houses all over the country. Ultimately he was seen as the undisputed authority in the knowledge of how tobacco could be grown, how to judge it when it was ready for sale, how to handle it, and how to buy and sell it.[4]

His mastery of the tobacco world led Clarence LeBus to the leadership position in the epic struggles of the small-time Kentucky tobacco farmers against the oppressive dictates imposed by James Duke and his American Tobacco Company. Duke's use of his tobacco monopoly gave him almost total control of the prices paid for tobacco. The farmers were forced into servitude-like conditions.⁵ What followed was the titanic clash of two iron-willed giants, James Duke of the American tobacco Company and Clarence LeBus of Cynthiana, Kentucky, and the sometimes nightmarish circumstances accompanying the struggle for a fair price.

The magnitude of the influence of burley tobacco to the farming in central and north central Kentucky during the early 20th century cannot be overstated. A close look at this culture and its evolution is prerequisite to a meaningful understanding of the life of Clarence LeBus and the Tobacco Wars of 1900-1909.

Tobacco was indigenous to the American Continents. Several different varieties were smoked and chewed extensively by the Native Americans. Christopher Columbus and his shipmates were introduced to the weed in their first days of exploring the newly discovered lands. These Europeans found smoking the plant to be quite pleasurable. They were impressed. On March 15, 1493 Columbus made his return to Spain. He had samples of what he considered to be riches to demonstrate the great potential of the lands he had explored. His samples included gold, several Native American people, exotic birds, and tobacco. Smoking was not a European endeavor until that moment, and the practice quickly became a fad and spread in popularity.⁶

Smoking tobacco in pipes became the new "cool" throughout Europe, and the demand for American tobacco grew exponentially. Eventually, tobacco became the number one commodity exported from the Americas to Europe. The accounts of the introduction of tobacco into Europe are somewhat vague and sometimes conflicting. That Columbus and his companions acquired the custom of smoking it and carried the custom back to Europe, there can be little doubt. Tobacco became more generally known and used in the Americas after the settlements of Roanoke Island in 1585 and Jamestown in 1607. The tobacco used in America and the tobacco sent to Europe between the time of Columbus and the

Roanoke and Jamestown settlements was harvested from the plantings of the Native Americans and what, if any, could be found growing wild. One of the first people to recognize the value and potential of tobacco was John Rolfe. He came to Jamestown (in what is now Virginia) in 1610 and began to grow tobacco on the land he had cleared. It is important to note the fact that John Rolfe married Pocahontas, because this union enabled him to get the very best tobacco seeds from his father-in-law's imperial stores. He did so well financially on his third crop in 1614 that he was able to afford a journey to England with his wife. In England, John Rolfe introduced his wife, the former Pocahontas, to London society, and this so impressed the other colonists that they began to grow tobacco on every available piece of land, including the streets of Jamestown.[7]

Beginning with the year 1620, at least 100,000 pounds of Virginia tobacco were shipped to England annually. The weed was so valuable that it became legal tender. One hundred and fifty years later in 1790, and in the lifetime of George Washington, the annual tobacco crop amounted to 130 million pounds. Three unique features guaranteed tobacco's growth and perpetuation: it was pleasurable, it became fashionable and a fad, and it was addictive.

In the early 1770s when Daniel Boone and Simon Kenton were wandering around exploring what is now Kentucky, they were the only humans in the area that weren't indigenous to the place. But, settlement came quickly: Boonesborough was founded in 1775, and a short eighteen years later, the city of Cynthiana was founded in 1793.[8]

The migration westward can be attributed primary to three factors. First was the natural inclination of people to move and to seek out new territories. Secondly, Boone, Kenton, and others propagated glowing stories of the riches and beauty to be found in the new lands just over the mountains.[9] And thirdly, there was the pressure created by the ever increasing population in the east. In addition, the poor farming habits of the Virginia planters had so impoverished the soil that there was a persistent zeal for fresh tobacco lands, and that sent the planters farther and farther westward.[10]

The first settlers moving into Kentucky were usually men traveling alone. Their intentions were to find a place to clear and farm, build some shelter or cabin, and send for their families later. They needed very little: their pack horse and a rifle, gun powder and lead, ax and adze. Knives, steel traps, rope, iron pots, salt, and seeds were also usually packed. Later, after the arrival of their families, a patch of corn and a garden were put out. Some tobacco was usually grown, but it was only a few plants for personal consumption. These early Kentucky farmers were very much living lives of isolation and subsistence. They were dependent upon little more than what they could get through their own initiatives.[11]

Food was not a big problem for the earliest residents of Kentucky. Sources of protein were almost unlimited. A look at the map today reveals just how many places were named for elk, deer, hickories and walnuts. The streams were teeming with easy-to-catch fish. There was little need for a cash crop, and that need was usually met by the enterprise of trapping. The furs of the beavers, otters, minks, and muskrats were traded for staples at the trading posts and stores that were soon in the settlements.

Kentucky in 1792 had a population of 100,000. The influx of people moving into Kentucky almost doubled on a yearly basis. In fact, the increase of Kentucky's population was an object of wonder and even jealousy to the eastern states. In seventeen years it had increased from nothing to over 100,000. No other state in the union had experienced such growth. Before 1780 the population had not numbered more than a few hundred, but that year saw the beginning of the great migration from Virginia. Three years later, it was estimated that Kentucky contained 12,000 people; by 1784 the number had become 20,000; by 1790 73,000 and by 1792 the population was 100,000. This population was confined almost wholly to the Bluegrass area and the hillsides of the Outer Bluegrass. Very small rural communities prevailed. There was no town in Kentucky numbering more than 1,000 inhabitants. In 1790 Lexington contained 834; Washington 462; Louisville 350; and Danville 150. Cynthiana, the future home of Clarence LeBus, was home to about one hundred people. Boonesborough was still one of the thriving towns of Kentucky, and Maysville was bidding to become the metropolis of the west.[12]

The added population put tremendous pressure on the availability of game for food and on the fur bearing animals to trap. It became increasingly more difficult to find both. This combination of more people and less readily available food put a subtle pressure on the inhabitants: they had to eat, and cash was needed to both acquire the necessary tools to grow and preserve the food and to buy what they couldn't grow as well.

Since tobacco was a crop that could not be largely consumed by the producer, and it was practically impossible to get it to the existing markets in the east because of distance and poor transportation, the result was that very little was raised; and those tiny crops were almost solely for the farmer's personal use. There was an existing warehouse in Louisville that was erected in 1783; but since Spain controlled New Orleans and the lower Mississippi River, there was no viable way to get the Kentucky crops to the markets in the eastern states or to Europe. It was in the year 1787 that James Wilkinson, formerly a Revolutionary War General, left Louisville with two flatboats loaded with tobacco, bacon, and flour. After his boats were seized and then released, he negotiated a deal with the Spanish to become an agent. Growth in the amount of tobacco raised in Kentucky was immediately sparked by the fact that the tobacco that brought two dollars per hundredweight in Louisville was bringing ten dollars in New Orleans. The opening of the markets in New Orleans enabled the Kentucky settlers to shift from furs, timber, and game to the growing of small amounts of tobacco to serve as a cash crop.[13]

Tobacco as a crop was especially accommodating to the vast woodlands of Kentucky since it required small patches that could be hacked out of the forests. A large yield per acre, as well as the close care and supervision required, has always confined tobacco to a relatively small plot of farm land. The small hill farms that were prevalent in the areas north, south, and east of the inner bluegrass were perfect for tobacco production: the flat land for crops was mostly limited to ridge tops and narrow creek bottoms. By the 1860s, almost every farm in the area was producing some tobacco.

Agents were there to buy the crops directly off the farms, and large tobacco markets were initially in Louisville and Cincinnati. Soon they were commonplace around the state. There was no problem getting the tobacco sold. When the farmers received cash from their small crops and were faced with a slight surplus of money, their standards of living increased, and their needs advanced to include kerosene, material for clothes, sugar, flour, nails, paper, and more.

By the time of Clarence LeBus' youth, tobacco was a big deal. The big farms of the Bluegrass and the river-bottom farms of the hill country used tenants to produce large amounts of the plant. The small family farms were growing an acre or two. From the beginning to the end, the labor requirements were huge. The small farmer rarely raised a crop without the help of neighbors.[14]

Tobacco was a labor intensive, hands-on, crop. The work began in the dead of winter when the farmer began to gather wood to "burn" the tobacco beds. Limbs, small logs, dead-falls and sticks were gathered up and stacked in a line where the seed beds were to be plowed, harrowed, and raked. When the weather was right, the wood was set on fire and very slowly drug across the long narrow 100 x 12 feet seed beds. This was an all day long job, and it was standard practice for the wives and sisters of the workers to bring lunch to the men, because it was one job that they could not leave. "Burning" the tobacco beds sterilized the soil and killed what would be competing weed seeds. The tobacco seeds were so small that they had to be diligently mixed with sand and then broadcast over the sterile beds. A thin cotton fabric was then stretched over the bed to protect the plants from frost and wind-blown weed seeds after they emerged.

Before mechanization, the farmer had to till the soil designated for the crop either with hand tools or with horse or mule-drawn equipment. When the soil was in good shape, and after the danger of frost, the mature plants had to be "pulled" by hand from the plant beds and set out in the prepared fields. Most generally, some family members or neighbors would be pulling the plants while others were in the fields setting the plants in the long rows where they would remain and grow until late summer or early fall. Both pulling the plants and setting them by hand were back-breaking jobs.

Throughout the summer the farmer had to "chop out" the long rows, using a hand held garden hoe to kill the emerging weeds. Green tobacco worms had to be continuously removed from the plants. Late in the summer secondary growths called "suckers" began to grow where the leaves met the stem. The "suckers" had to be broken off and removed by hand. Finally, the tops of each plant had to be broken off. Both the "topping" and the "suckering" promoted the growth of the leaves.

Sometime before the first of September 30th (the date used to signal the time of the first potential frost), the crop had to be cut and "housed." The men, and sometimes women, cut the mature plant at the base, speared it onto a tobacco stick, and hung the sticks in a barn to "cure." After about six weeks, when the leaves were deemed to be "in case," the sticks were "dropped" and carried to the "stripping room" where the leaves were removed from the stalks and tied into "hands" in accordance with their perceived "grade." The crop was then ready for sale, and it was almost time for the farmer to start over again.

In the late nineteenth and early twentieth century, the conversations at the general store, at the blacksmith shop, in a chance meeting on the road, or at the dinner table, would always turn to tobacco. Who had good crops, who had problems, the prospects for a good sale price, and the weather were always important things to pass along. The first days of sales were celebrated. Community events, fairs and parades had tobacco themes. The merchants, doctors, lawyers, and equipment dealers began to bill the farmers on an annual basis, and of course those bills were due when the crops were sold. Often, the banks and merchants financed the farmers' crops for the upcoming crop-year. Without doubt, in rural Kentucky the tobacco crop was of the utmost importance to almost everyone.

Chapter Three

In 1877, Clarence's older brother, Orie, accepted a position working away from the farm. Their father, Lewis, offered Orie a deal in an attempt to instill in the young man a feeling for the importance of saving his money. The terms were that the father would match whatever Orie saved in a six month period. Orie was able to save a considerable amount of what he earned, and Lewis did, in fact, pay the young man.

Two years later, trained in practical farm duties, and upon the advice of his father who wanted to see the younger brother, Clarence, broaden his training, the young man accepted a clerkship in a general merchandise store in the village of Havlandsville, Kentucky. Clarence was seventeen years old. His salary was fifteen per month, board and laundry. When the time came for Clarence to leave home and try his fortune at fifteen per month, he asked his father if the deal he had made with Orie would be duplicated. Lewis LeBus didn't hesitate before replying to his son, "Yes, but there is no need to wait to see what you will save in six months. We all know you'll not spend a cent. Here is your $90."[1]

Clarence LeBus was born on a farm near Oddville Kentucky on December 29, 1862. He was the second child in a family of seven children. At that time, the community of Oddville was a tiny settlement about six miles northeast of the town of Cynthiana. Oddville was originally named Mt. Washington, but the local preacher decided to change the name to Oddville when the post office was installed, because the name Mt. Washington was already taken. He believed that Oddville was a peculiar little community, and so he gave it that name. Actually, there was nothing "odd" about the place. During Clarence's early childhood, Oddville consisted of one church, one school, two stores, a mill, a blacksmith and five or six houses. It was, in fact, much like every other small community in Kentucky. There were small farms, rolling hills, creeks, and woodlands.

Clarence LeBus's childhood activities were much like those of all the boys of rural Kentucky. They began to work at an early age. They had daily "chores" that they were responsible for, and they worked in the fields along with the adult men. The boys fished, hunted, attended church, and went to school when they could. But Clarence LeBus's family circumstances were a little different than most of the boys in the Oddville neighborhood.

Clarence's mother, Martha Garrett, was the granddaughter of Reverend Josiah Whitaker, and around Oddville Kentucky in the 1860s that was a big deal. Whitaker was a Revolutionary War veteran who received the land grant in 1799 that allowed him to own about one thousand acres that included the area that would become Oddville. The decedents of Josiah Whitaker all settled around the Oddville crossroads, and, to some degree, their kinship to the man gave them a unique status.

Certainly, Clarence LeBus's father, Lewis LeBus, was an extraordinary man with extraordinary abilities. In addition to his thrift and agricultural abilities, he was a shrewd businessman who was evidently liked by all and sought out for his advice.[2] When the Civil War broke out, he furnished horses to the government for the much needed Calvary service. During that same time, he was appointed to the office of Sheriff of Harrison County, and he became the Internal Revenue Collector for the Covington District. On top of this he found huge success buying and selling stocks and bonds. Lewis LeBus's non-agricultural activities did not keep his attention away from livestock raising, tobacco production and land buying; farming was always his main interest. He believed that land that was bought was to be kept and not sold. Ultimately he owned one thousand acres of the finest bluegrass farmland, as well as land in Alabama, Ohio, and California.[3]

Lewis LeBus, himself a school teacher, had a brother, Joseph, who reached the pinnacle in the education circles. Joseph LeBus was educated in Ohio and graduated from Saint Vincent's College at the head of his class in 1852. He taught at numerous public and private schools in Ohio and northern Kentucky as well as at the Oddville School. He lived with Lewis and his wife during the unrest of the Civil War and visited with extended stays on several occasions. He became the Superintendent of the Harrison County School System and was responsible for bringing all the local schools under the supervision of one central office. Joseph settled in Harrison County and remained close to his brother, Lewis.[4] Clarence LeBus himself attended the University of Michigan for two years. One of his sisters, Bertha, graduated from Wellesley College and became a lawyer; and another sister, Leona, graduated from Heidelberg College of Ohio and Johns Hopkins Medical School.[5] It's easy to see that the entire LeBus family put an extraordinary emphasis on the importance of education.

Unlike most of the boys in the small hill-farm communities of northern and north-central Kentucky, the LeBus brothers were sent to school even when there was work to do on the farm. The common practice in the area was that work came before school when it meant getting the tobacco crop in, but with Lewis LeBus's sons the reverse was true.

It was here; as a boy on his father's farm, living in a rational, thrifty, and frugal family that Clarence and his siblings spent their days of youth. One has to believe that Clarence and his brother, Orie, experienced the usual older brother/younger brother family dynamics. What we do know for sure is that the two remained very close throughout their adult lives.

Clarence and Orie spent a great deal of time with their father both at home and at work wherever the work might have been. Either through inheritance or through the influence of experience, Clarence began to show his father's marked ability and unusual taste for business. He was demonstrating an intelligence, sagacity, energy, and thrift at an early age, and one has to wonder if the remarkable career of the adult Clarence LeBus could have been seen in the boy.[6]

Young Clarence LeBus began working in earnest when he was ten years old. He was hired by neighbors to pick off the suckers that sprouted between the leaves and the stalks of the tobacco plants. Lewis Lebus believed that his children benefited from whatever new experiences they could have with people and work, and all of his sons were encouraged to work off the farm when the opportunity presented itself.[7]

At age twelve Clarence began working as a hand in the tobacco fields of neighbors for fifty cents per day. The work was hard, and the hours long, but even at this early age Clarence LeBus seemed driven to earn, and more importantly, to save. It was about this time that Clarence began experimenting with other money-making projects. He began by raising cabbage, turning it into sauerkraut, and selling it.[8] His time was consumed with these activities: traveling with his father, attending school, and working on and off the farm.

Clarence attended the local public school in Oddville through the sixth grade. He had a particular aptitude for mathematics. Next, his father sent him to Smith's Academy in Cynthiana to complete his secondary education.[9] Smith's Academy was a private school with a good reputation and a certain prestige. It was a small school of about ten students and satisfied the county's need for a high school: there was no public high school in the county at that time. Some of the students came from away and boarded at the school. It is not known if Clarence LeBus made the daily trip from Oddville to Cynthiana, or if he stayed at the school.

It was during the summer following his graduation from the Academy that he took the job at the general mercantile store at Havlandsville. He was seventeen years old at the time. The job paid fifteen dollars per month, and he was given a place to live in the back of the store. The store owner provided meals and laundry service as well. The fifteen dollars that he earned each month equates to about $400 per month at today's values. He evidently applied himself to the job in an impressive manner, as he was asked by the owner to continue for another year at double the salary with an interest in the company.[10]

Clarence LeBus turned down the job promotion and instead enrolled at The University of Michigan. Enrollment to any university would have been unusual for a young man living in rural Kentucky at that time, but attendance to the University of Michigan would have been almost unheard of. Clarence attended the university and excelled in the study of mathematics and engineering until halfway through his sophomore year when he had to quit because of poor eyesight. He had always had difficulty with his eyes, but he had been able to overcome it until faced with the rigors of hours and hours of reading and studying.[11]

Upon his return to Cynthiana (Lewis LeBus had moved his family to Cynthiana), Clarence considered his formal education complete. He entered the world of work full-time. He was twenty years old.

Setting Tobacco in Kentucky, circa 1900

AN IRON-WILLED GIANT

Hauling the tobacco crop to the barn, Harrison County, Kentucky, circa 1900

Chapter Four

James Buchanan Duke was a man of extraordinary abilities. He was blessed with a keen mind and an unyielding drive. He could work day after day with little or no rest. He grew from poverty after the Civil war to become one of the wealthiest men in the United States. Through untiring effort and application of keen organizational skills, he eventually owned one of the historic mega monopolies: the American Tobacco Company.

In the year 1914, Clinton W. Toms, president of the Liggett and Myers Company, said of James Duke:[1]

> His power of concentration – his ability to put into any one task his whole power and then turn around and do the same thing with an entirely different problem.
>
> His enthusiasm-not the hurrah kind, but the intelligent forceful expression of a great personality.
>
> His faculty of putting emphasis where it belonged, readily discerning between the essential and the nonessential.
>
> His power to inspire men to be something and to do something, creating within them a real ambition to succeed. Often by praise and then again by fair and just criticism, even though at times it might be severe, he enabled men to overcome a weakness and then they were grateful to him.
>
> His consideration for men – those who worked under him were always given more than due credit, and his desire that those who tried to do their part should be liberally rewarded.

His big-bigheartedness – a kind and sympathetic nature.

His great faith – a genuine faith – a strong confidence in the Christian religion. (Sic)

———◆———

In October, 1905 Clarence LeBus went to New York for an interview with James Duke, president of The American Tobacco Company. He told Mr. Duke that tobacco tenants could not live on the prevailing prices. Mr. Duke declared that he could do nothing to give relief. Mr. LeBus then declared that the days of domination by the American Tobacco Company in Kentucky were numbered. He said the African slaves had been freed, the turnpikes were freed from the unfair toll-gates, and he declared his belief that the white tobacco tenant farmer would find relief. Mr. Duke assumed a look of disdain and skeptically inquired how LeBus thought that change could be brought about. Mr. LeBus' replied: "I do not know. It may be by the ballot, it may be by legislation, it may be in the courts, and it may be at the muzzle of the shotgun. I cannot say how, but the people of Kentucky will not much longer tolerate your methods of oppression that are impoverishing them while you enjoy enormous profits."[2]

———◆———

On an old farm near the tiny community of Durham, North Carolina, on December 23, 1856, James Buchanan Duke was born. He was the son of Washington Duke and Artelia Roney Duke. James was the youngest of five children. The family was considered to be "good people," and Washington Duke had the respect of everyone.

The large family of five children and two adults meant that every member was accustomed to hard work from childhood. They didn't mind that; it was all they knew. All farmers' children worked.

The Dukes were far from rich, and there were times when mere survival was the goal. Their neighbors were no better off and in many cases were not as fortunate as the Dukes.

Washington Duke recalled that he grew up in a section where there were no extremes of poverty or wealth. What he meant by that was that everyone had food, clothing, and shelter, but beyond that, life was hard. Lack of transportation brought certain isolation to the people of the Piedmont region of North Carolina; the rivers were not navigable, and railroads did not arrive until after mid-century. With the isolation came a certain degree of hardship. The nearest true town was Hillsborough, and it was twelve miles from the Duke home.

Given such isolation, Washington Duke really had no other options but to spend his early years behind the plow. He received only a few months of formal education which allowed him to sign his name, and that was about it. For several years prior to his eighteenth birthday he lived and farmed with an older brother. It was about the year 1838 that Washington Duke began to farm on his own.

The fathers of both James Duke and Clarence LeBus seemed to share some life-defining characteristics. Both Washington Duke and Lewis LeBus were big strong men who were able and willing to work and labor for hours on end. They were both very frugal and used that thrift as a method to improve their circumstances. And, while LeBus had certain education and Washington had little or none, both men believed in the importance of formal education and emphasized it to their children.

Working diligently and living frugally, Washington Duke first farmed on rented land. When he married Mary Clinton in 1842, her father gave them a small parcel of farmland. Washington managed through his work and thrift to add to the holdings, and by the outbreak of the civil war he owned over three hundred acres. He was able to grow enough wheat and corn to supplement the hogs and cattle that were used for pork, beef, and milk. Chickens and turkeys added to the provender with eggs and meat. The family was able to raise enough cotton and tobacco to provide a little cash in the fall to buy the things that couldn't be raised on the farm.

Washington Duke's life and plans were abruptly changed when the civil war broke out. Wash, as he was called, was not at all sympathetic to the secessionists. He thought the war was a mistake that would lead to tragedy for all. Though unhappy about a war that he and others did not want, Washington Duke made preparations late in 1863 to join the Confederate Service when the government moved to draft men up to forty-five years of age. As a twice-widowed father who had a teen-aged son and three young children to care for, he no doubt resented the necessity that confronted him; but he had no choice.

The farmer-turned-soldier auctioned off his livestock, wagons, and other supplies, left his children with the parents of his then deceased second wife (James Duke was eight years old at that time), and in 1864 he joined the confederate army. Washington was transferred several times and served as a private and ultimately a Sergeant in North Carolina, South Carolina, and Virginia. Ultimately he was captured by the Federals during the confusion that accompanied Lee's withdrawal from Richmond. He was sent to Libby Prison a week before Lee's surrender. He was paroled a few weeks later, sent by ship to New Bern, and then had to walk the 130 miles to his home.[3]

James Duke was nine years old when his father returned from the war. Until then he had been mostly incubated from the horrors and tragedies of the bloody war as he whiled away those turbulent years at his grandparent's home. A gaunt and shabbily dressed Washington Duke had walked for weeks to get home. The journey was difficult: whatever food he ate was shared with him by people who were no better off than himself. After the difficult journey, he arrived at his in-law's, visited and rested for a short time, and then gathered his children up and headed to his old farm.

When he stood and surveyed the place, it must have been devastating to him. Almost everything was gone. The Union soldiers had helped themselves to whatever they needed or wanted, and what they didn't take was removed by others and the theft blamed on the soldiers from the north. There were no harnesses, no saddles, no tools or equipment- nothing! The house was emptied of everything except for some people living there who claimed to have some title. The picture was not encouraging. The outlook for mere survival was bleak. But Washington Duke's Yankee enemies had left one thing untouched. The tobacco barn was still full of the last year's crop, hanging just as it was left by whoever had housed it in the first place.[4]

Sometimes a small and seemly inconsequential happenstance can propagate a chain of events that ends with a staggering outcome, and that is exactly what the ignored tobacco did for the Duke family. A fifty cent piece was the extent of Wash Duke's working capital. He had swapped a five dollar confederate note with a Yankee trouper for the coin. His only other possession was a pair of blind mules that he either found in a field near his farm or were given to him when the war ended. Wash Duke saw the hanging tobacco, realized at once that it was his only hope for some immediate cash, and without hesitation he came up with a plan. At that moment, the Duke Tobacco Company was born.

Before the tobacco could be sold, it had to be processed and made ready to smoke. On the farm was an old log barn, and that became the Duke's first factory. They had no machinery, so the leaf had to be pulverized by hand. Children, father, and friends all helped with the job. Using flails, the tobacco was pulverized, sifted, and packaged in bags to be sold as pipe smoking tobacco. There was nothing fine or fancy about the process or the packing, but it was sound honest tobacco that made a good smoke. The amateur manufacturers created a brand of their own and boldly named it, "Pro Bono Publico" – For the Public Good.

Selling the smoking tobacco was the next problem. They loaded the sacked "Pro Bono" on an old borrowed covered wagon and hung a box that contained mostly borrowed pans, skillets, bacon, corn meal, blankets and everything else they would need for an extended trip into the countryside and then headed to the southern part of the state where tobacco was scarce. The two old and blind mules provided the power for the wagon. Washington Duke and his son, James, followed the dirt roads from one tiny community to the next. They stopped at every crossroad store they passed and let go with their sales pitch. When they ran into strangers along the way, they too became targets of their sales efforts. The amateur merchants did well along their route, and the unusual crew proved one thing to themselves: they were good salesmen. When the prospects could not pay in cash, things that could be used or sold later were taken in barter. In addition to earning a little cash, the adventurers were gaining friends and customers for the future.

The tobacco was sold faster than they imagined, and with some of the cash Washington Duke bought a quantity of bacon. He then traded two barrels of flour that they had taken in barter for two hundred pounds of cotton that he sold when they reached Raleigh. He bought a bag of brown sugar to take home to the children. They headed home with bacon, a sack of candy (sugar), and money in their hands. Having some money was surely a powerful emotional event; there just wasn't any cash in the south after the Civil War.

The excursion was a financial success for the Dukes and was followed by many others. Washington Duke knew the fickle nature of raising a crop of tobacco. It was a lengthy process that took almost the entire year. Profit depended upon quality, and quality depended upon skill, talent, and mostly luck. Drought, a rain soaked season, or an irregular curing season could turn a year's work into ruin. Washington Duke decided after the successful sales event, and with the input from his young sons, to let other farmers raise the tobacco. They would sell it. From that time on tobacco crops grown on the Duke farms were small and inconsequential.

When the sales runs began, James B. Duke was nine years old; but he was energetic and somewhat wise for his age. The period was romantic as well as arduous for the young man. Sleeping under the stars, cooking and eating with his father, and discussing every move with him were the daily fare. Their relationship became symbiotic: the elder Duke benefiting from the young man's energy and creative way of seeing things, and young James Duke soaking up his father's wisdom. They made a formidable combination.

By the time James Duke was ten years old, he and his older brother, Ben, had almost total responsibility for the Duke farms. Ben was two years older than James, but they were inseparable throughout their lives. The remarkable career of James and the spectacular growth of the American Tobacco Company only strengthened their close relationship. It was when the two boys were at a very early age that James began to assume the role of "big brother."

Although every member of the Duke family worked hard, "Old Wash" was insistent that they all attained more education than he had. An aunt probably taught the children to read and write; and during the slack work periods, but only during the slack periods, they attended the academy at Durham. Washington sent the girls off to the school that later became Guilford College. When it came time for James to go to the same school, he decided that he was not enchanted with literary studies, missed the farm and the work, and came home before the semester was half over. James was always quick with his school work, particularly so in mathematics, but he was a terrible student, who only about halfway attended. Considering the likelihood that he was not going to succeed at college, it was not difficult for him to talk his father into letting him attend a session at Eastman Business College in Poughkeepsie, New York. It was there that he was taught basic bookkeeping skills and rudimentary accounting. James Duke was about seventeen years old at the time of his stay in Poughkeepsie. Washington Duke wanted his children to go to college, but James would have none of it; nor would he ever admit that a college education would have benefited him in any way. Later in life, he was quoted thus: "College is all right for teachers and preachers, but what good would an education be to me?"[5]

It is important to note that, while Washington saw the benefits of education, his perception of what an education meant was pale when compared to the emphasis that the family of Clarence Lebo's put on formal and classical education. Ultimately this difference could have contributed to the outcomes of the burley tobacco wars.

James Duke's oldest brother "Brodie" did not join the rest of the family in the tobacco manufacturing business at first. He decided to work the family farm, but after one year of unrelenting work and hardly any profit, he too joined the business. Washington Duke continued to take the blind mule-driven wagon on the road peddling the smoking tobacco, and the brothers stayed back and ran the farm and their manufacturing business. In less than a year, it was necessary to build a bigger barn to process the tobacco. Before the year 1866 was out, that barn also had become too small. They moved their operation into an abandoned house, but it was also quickly outgrown. Washington Duke and his sons decided at that time they should build an appropriate building to house their rapidly growing business, and they did. The building was similar to other farm/factories throughout the south that were manufacturing plug and smoking tobacco. In the year of 1866, the Dukes manufactured 15,000 pounds of smoking tobacco. In 1877, Washington Duke sold his farm and moved his family to Durham; there they built a new frame factory building.

Durham acquired its first tobacco-auction warehouse in 1871. It was a huge success from the beginning. The farmers delivered their crop to the warehouse, and it was sold mostly to middlemen who then resold to the manufacturers. James Duke immediately began to utilize the auction sales to buy the tobacco that was needed to run the Duke factory. He became somewhat of an expert in appraising and judging the leaf at a very early age.[6] As the family business grew and ultimately became an integral part of the American Tobacco Company, he continued the practice of buying tobacco leaf directly from the warehouse sales. This meant he was bypassing a large number of speculative middlemen, and that caused great friction within the industry. Duke believed correctly that his methods were the most economical and added the most to his bottom line. Ultimately he was buying so much tobacco that it was putting the middlemen out of business. When they complained, he said, "It's not my concern."

Although W. Duke and Sons was clearly doing a modestly successful business by 1880, they were only one of about a dozen tobacco manufacturers in Durham. The firm that loomed far above all the others was the Blackwell Company that made the world famous Bull Durham smoking tobacco. The Bull Durham factory then became the largest tobacco manufacturing company in the world. It was in 1881, that the Blackwell Company built a huge new brick factory equipped with the most expensive equipment on the market.[7]

James Duke, then twenty-five years old and clearly the boss of the Duke business, could see what was ahead: they could not compete with the huge companies and expect to grow. He decided that they should go into the cigarette business. The smoking tobacco they were all producing was not cigarette tobacco; it was for smoking in pipes. The cigarette business, as such, was in its infancy in the United States.

Popular in the Spanish speaking parts of the world, cigarettes did not appear widely in other world places until the 1850s. Immigrants and rich Americans who could afford to travel in Europe helped introduce the new fad into the United States, and by 1864 the manufacture of cigarettes had begun in New York City. That is where cigarette smoking first caught on, and from there the practice began to spread throughout the United States.[8]

The major expense in manufacturing cigarettes in 1881 was not the tobacco, but the cost of making them. Cigarettes in the 1880s had to be hand rolled: there was no machinery to make them. Initially, skilled hand rollers had to be brought over from Europe to train American workers. When the Duke Company began cigarette production in 1881, James Duke arranged for skilled cigarette makers from New York, most of them Jewish immigrants from Eastern Europe, to be brought to his factory. Eventually, but only temporarily, more than 100 such hand-rollers worked in the Duke factory.[9]

In the first year of serious cigarette production the W. Duke and Sons Tobacco Company made and sold 9 million cigarettes. While this is an impressive number for an upstart cigarette maker, it pales when compared to the 384 million cigarettes made in New York during the same year. In order to increase production, James Duke needed more revenue, but he was adverse to borrowing money. Initially, two partnerships were sold, and the much needed revenue was obtained. For the most part, these new partners were energetic, capable and contributed a great deal to the expansion of the company. It was then that the W. Duke and Sons Tobacco Company became a partnership.

In 1885 James Bonsack of Virginia invented a cigarette-making machine, and James Duke took a huge gamble and persuaded his partners to give the new machine more than a casual try. W. Duke and Sons would be the first cigarette manufacturer in America to take such a step. The machine could in theory make as many cigarettes in one day as forty-eight skilled hand rollers. There were two big obstacles blocking widespread acceptance of the machine: first, it worked only sporadically and sometimes not at all; and second, there was a widespread belief among the manufacturers that smokers preferred hand-rolled cigarettes.

Despite these problems, Duke and Sons installed the first Bonsack machine in their Durham factory in 1884. The Bonsack Machine Company leased the machines on a royalty basis of approximately two-thirds of the cost of hand rolling the cigarettes. The company provided the machine and an operator and charged thirty-three cents per thousand for the cigarettes produced. A stroke of good luck fell upon the Duke Company when Bonsack sent William T. O'Brian to work on the machine as a mechanic. It turned out that O'Brian was an extremely capable mechanic. He kept tinkering with the machine in a non-stop effort to get it to operate properly. Over time he was able to do what nobody else had been able to do: he got the Bonsack Cigarette Machine to operate perfectly. O'Brian became a long-term employee of the company.

The reluctance of the other major cigarette producers to go to the Bonsack machine opened the way for Duke to make a move that would ultimately give him a competitive edge. James Duke entered into an agreement with Bonsack Company whereas Duke agreed to phase out all hand-rollers and go exclusively to using the Bonsack machines. Bonsack then agreed that W. Duke and Sons would forever be charged a rate of twenty-five cents per thousand cigarettes while all others would be held to the thirty-three cents charge per thousand. Bonsack also agreed that they would not lease the machines to any company other than Duke's and the other four top cigarette producers. It was a gamble, but a good deal for both of them: Bonsack got their machine in use in the United States, and Duke got, while not a complete monopoly, a huge competitive advantage.

The deal with Bonsack put Duke exactly where he thought it would. Eventually the machines worked so well that the other companies had to abandon the hand-rolling and go to the Bonsack. The deal that James Duke had struck with Bonsack meant a perpetual obstacle for the others to overcome in order to compete. W. Duke and Sons had a huge advantage in any price war that might ensue, and James Duke was not reluctant to use it. In addition, as the competition stiffened, the advertising costs also skyrocketed. James Duke was systematically destroying his competition. When James Duke proposed the merger of W. Duke and Sons with the four largest other cigarette producers, their drive for survival insured that the four got on board.

The American Tobacco Company was formed in 1890 when the W. Duke and Sons Company merged with the Ginter, Kimball, Kinney, and Goodwin Companies. Of course Duke maintained the largest share. James W. Duke had muscled his way to become the head of the largest cigarette/tobacco company in America. The five firms combined controlled between 90 and 95 percent of the paper cigarette business in the United States, and that meant, of course, that they would be buying 90 to 95 percent of the tobacco that went into making the cigarettes.

On the other hand, almost all of the white burley tobacco needed to make cigarettes was raised in and around central Kentucky. Looking back, it's easy to see that these circumstances created a situation ripe for a showdown.

Chapter Five

> From The Anderson News, Lawrenceburg, KY. June 21 1928.
>
> The story of the life of Clarence LeBus reads like a romance. It is one of sterling integrity in the face of great temptation.

> From The Commercial Tribune, Cincinnati, Ohio. November 7, 1909. (Reported as a quote that Mr. LeBus often spoke regarding caution when it came to spending money)
>
> Watch the little dime leaks that dollars won't fit through.

Clarence LeBus was a serious student at the University of Michigan during the years of 1880-1882. Unfortunately fate would not allow his academic quest to continue through to graduation. LeBus had dealt with mild diabetes during his childhood, but the disease didn't hamper him much until he faced the rigors of study at the university level. It was then that his failing eyesight became too much. He left the University in the winter of 1882 and returned home to Cynthiana at the age of twenty. Up until the moment of his leaving, LeBus had been an exemplary student of mathematics and engineering at the University. He had always had a knack for numbers and mathematics, and that was a gift that stayed with him throughout his life.

The personal growth and wealth of Clarence LeBus was spectacular between the time of his return from the University of Michigan in 1882 and his election as President of the Burley Tobacco Society on January 1, 1907. He went from a frugal, hard-working, educated young man with a savings of about $1,000 to become one of the wealthiest men in America at the young age of forty five. The 1907 date marked the end of one lifestyle for LeBus and the beginning of another. It was at that time that he was chosen to lead the farmers in their grueling struggle fighting the cruel and oppressive monopoly of James Duke and his American Tobacco Company.

Clarence's father was forty-six years old when Clarence returned home from Ann Arbor. Lewis had reached the pinnacle of farming and investment accomplishment in rural Kentucky. His farm holdings numbered over 2,000 acres. He was the largest landowner in Harrison County, and the land that he owned was viewed to be the very best. While Clarence was at the university, Lewis moved his family to a magnificent 500 acre river bottom farm known then as the Walton Farm (Today the farm is known as the A-Keller Farm.) The move put them much closer to town, and they were then living in a large and spacious house.[1]

While it is impossible to know what Clarence LeBus's career objectives had been when he entered the University of Michigan to study mathematics, it's not hard to imagine that, to an excellent life-long student, the health issue and the accompanying end of his academic career would have presented him with the need for certain adjustments. What is known is that when Clarence returned home to Kentucky he began to vigorously involve himself with his father's farming and business activities, but this work was also short lived. Both endeavors required strenuous physical activity, and once again fate intervened: young Clarence abruptly fell into a long period of ill health. It is not known for sure exactly what his conditions were, but it has always been assumed that his illness was also connected to his diabetes. What is known is that physical labor was not an option. Fortunately, he was able to get around, take a job off the farm, and continue his habit of saving every penny he could.[2]

History best remembers Clarence LeBus for his all-out involvement in the battle between The American Tobacco Company and the Kentucky tobacco farmers, and his remarkable successes in farming and business are often overlooked. In fact, his business/farming accomplishments were remarkable.

Upon his return to Cynthiana, his previous employer W.D.Hickman at the Havlandsville Mercantile store immediately offered Clarence his old position back, but Clarence was not interested. Instead he went to work at a job where he could utilize his mathematics skills and where he could see more and learn more. In the spring of 1882, LeBus took a job working for the Internal Revenue collectors office.[3] This position allowed Clarence to utilize his education and his math skills, and in hindsight the work rendered much more than just that.

Clarence LeBus's work as a tax collector involved more than sitting in an office and waiting for people to come in to pay their back taxes. The young man's responsibilities included traveling around not only his home county but to the counties to the north and east of Harrison County as well. At the time, tax collectors traveled frequently. They were called upon to go to people's homes, search for assets, determine the values of land and equipment, and investigate delinquent accounts.

The benefits of the new job for Clarence LeBus went beyond just the mechanics of collecting past due taxes. His travels through the nine-county tax district familiarized the young man with the total geography of the area. He would see close up the farmland, the hillsides, the bottoms, creeks, ridges and the crops. When out of the office, the young man would meet and converse with people at the country stores, the crossroads, and the backyards. The conversations would often turn to the conditions of the tobacco crops. He was asked to look at other farmers crops, and his suggestions were valued. Clarence LeBus was gaining a reputation as somewhat of an expert on all things related to tobacco. Not only was he learning from his experiences, but he was establishing a reputation and making connections that would define his future as well.

During the four years that LeBus worked as a tax collector, he continued to help his father when he could. His illness prevented Clarence from hard physical work for over a year, but it didn't impede his lifelong drive to work long hours. He continued to help his father by checking on the farms and crops before and after a day of taking care of his duties as tax collector, and his health soon improved. Clarence lived with his parents during this time, and of course he saved every penny he could.

Events would begin to unfold for Clarence that would broadly define his future. As is always the case, happenstance prevailed, but Clarence LeBus would prove to be a master of seizing opportunity. His abilities and ambitions made success probable.

In the year 1884 when Clarence was twent-two years old, his father, Lewis took an extended trip and visit to Europe. Of course he had to leave someone in charge of his farms and other businesses. Clarence was his choice. It was a huge responsibility for the young man, but it didn't seem to faze Clarence. When Lewis returned he was a little surprised and exceedingly pleased with what he found. The excellent condition in which his father found his affairs upon his return showed how efficient his son had been.[4]

It is interesting that Orie LeBus was the older of the two LeBus boys, but Clarence was the son put in charge when Lewis left. It is not known where Orie was at that time or what exactly he was doing when his father left. What is known is that Orie was very capable and talented as well. All indications are that the bond between the two brothers was always strong: They partnered in numerous business and farming deals throughout their lives. The fact that Clarence was the son chosen to oversee his father's affairs (for whatever reason) gave the young man the chance to learn and to prove himself through that experience.

It is noteworthy that while taking care of his father's 2,000 acres and other businesses, he continued with his duties as tax collector. From his earliest days of work, Clarence LeBus was never engaged in just one job. He always had several business/farming deals going at one time.

In 1886, at age of twenty-four, Clarence left the Internal Revenue Service and took a job as a solicitor for the Bodmann

Warehouse Company of Cincinnati, Ohio.[5] At the time, Bodmann was the biggest buyer of tobacco in the central Kentucky area. The company bought the crops and then sold the tobacco in huge wooden barrels called hogsheads in the Louisville and Cincinnati markets. LeBus was paid sixty dollars per month. He provided his own horse and buggy.[6]

The Bodmann Company instructed Clarence LeBus what types (grades) of tobacco they wanted him to buy and how much he could offer for it. Clarence was to travel the countryside, visit the farms, judge the crops and make the purchases. The needs of the company would change frequently. They would buy certain grades of tobacco for short periods of time. They bought what they could sell and that was always changing. Burley tobacco today is cataloged basically into three grades, but in the 1880s there were seven or eight grades. The Bodmann Company needed an expert, and what they got in Clarence LeBus was just what they needed: an undisputed expert. LeBus's sharp eye for judging tobacco coupled with his advanced math skills made him a natural. It certainly helped that he seemed to have had a unending capacity for hard work.

It didn't take long for Clarence LeBus to gain the confidence of his supervisor H.H.Hoffman. Clarence was soon given the privilege of buying tobacco for himself while at the same time receiving a salary from the Bodmann Company. At this time Clarence was twenty-four years old and had saved the huge sum of $1,400 (this would equate to over $38,000 at today's values). With an eye for quality and color and good judgment of the value of tobacco, he invested his hard earned and carefully saved money in a few small crops, and the investments proved profitable. The year was 1887. From that time on, he would buy for the company the tobacco they needed and buy for himself other grades that he thought he could sell at a later time for profit. In the meantime, he continued to attract the attention of tobacco buyers and producers with his extraordinary knowledge concerning the quality of all the grades that were sold on the Cincinnati market.

The tobacco marketing business has never been without the reputation of being tainted with corruption. We don't know exactly where Clarence LeBus fit in this picture of business ethics, but all indications point to a man with unquestionable honesty and honorable conduct. What we know for sure is that he bought tobacco from farmers and sold it later for more than he paid for it. Was he able to sell the crops because he somehow had influence with the large companies buying tobacco? Did he take advantage of the farmer's lack of knowledge of what their crops were worth? Or did the farmers in fact benefit by his purchases because of his ability to sell the crops for more than they could have on their own. What is clear is that Clarence LeBus had the trust of the farmers. It appears he had a very solid reputation.

Buying tobacco became a driving force and defining characteristic in Clarence LeBus's success. For the remainder of his life he would buy tobacco that he judged to be in excellent shape and of a grade that he believed would soon be in high demand. He bought from farmers, agents, buyers and anywhere else he found it. He consolidated small purchases into increasingly larger and larger bundles. He might own as much as a million pounds of the leaf at one time. When the big buyers (including James Duke), were in the market for the varieties of tobacco that LeBus held, he would sell.

It was in this same year (1887) that Clarence bought his first farm. It was a small farm. He later testified that he lost $1,100 dollars the first year he owned the farm with a nonproductive tenant. It was not long before Clarence bought another farm.

LeBus's salary as a solicitor for Bodmann steadily rose over time. During the term of his employment with Bodmann Warehouse Company, his salary nearly tripled from the sixty dollars per month he earned when initially employed to $160 per month. In addition Bodmann began to pick up his expenses. He was employed by the warehouse company until 1900. It was then, after fourteen years with the company, that Clarence LeBus left the steady employ of Bodmann to take care of his own businesses. The Bodmann Company offered Clarence incentives to stay, but his holdings by then had grown to such an extent that managing them had become a full time job. He was thirty-eight years old.[7]

Between 1886 and 1900, and during the years of Clarence LeBus's employment as a tobacco solicitor, the young man did not have just one source of income: He had three. There was his salary from Bodmann, the profits he made from buying and selling tobacco for himself, and income from his farms. In addition to his sense of frugality and his drive to save every penny he could, his inclination to always have multiple sources of income was another characteristic he inherited from his father, Lewis LeBus. While both men were certainly farmers, they both always had sources of income in addition to what they made farming. At that time, most farmers were just farmers: It would have been unusual for a farmer to have a job off the farm. Lewis LeBus's practice had been to use whatever profits he made from farming to buy more farmland and not for living expenses. This practice tended to perpetuate itself as more land meant more income which meant more land. Young Clarence LeBus had adopted the same general principles.

From The Commercial Tribune, Cincinnati, Ohio. April 15, 1917

There are two kinds of wealth: wealth that is created and wealth that is acquired. The creator of wealth is a benefactor to mankind, while he who merely acquires wealth, is usually a detriment. A creator of wealth not only benefits himself but is the medium through which all those who come within the influence of his potentialities are in turn benefited.

That person who has no perspective beyond acquiring that which others have created, that seeks to collect, not to build up, seldom if ever confers a benefit upon any of his fellow creatures. The first is a philanthropist, the other a self-centered, sordid, grasping iconoclast. (sic)

The writer's message was clear: Clarence LeBus was of the first type. He was a creator of wealth, not a user of other people's resources.

> *From the St. Louis Commercial News, St. Louis, Missouri. Dec. 21, 1912.*
>
> He (LeBus) has little use for those who always start at the top of the ladder and are found at the bottom buried in the rubbish of failure.
>
> He has been a good climber and if one rung of the ladder breaks he grabs the side rails and gains the upper one. Energy does it and there is danger of falling. His faith in industry and energy never flags.

During the years between 1886 and 1890, Clarence bought, held, and sold increasingly larger amounts of tobacco with each passing year. It was risky business, but he was good at it. Clarence LeBus was accumulating significant wealth, and merely accumulating money no longer suited him. His small farm holdings were paying off as well, and beginning in the year 1890 he began to buy farmland aggressively. He adopted from his father the belief that farmland was not to be bought and sold, but was to be kept.[8] Clarence rarely sold a farm. When he did, it was to rid himself of land that he believed to be of lower quality. The farms he purchased were the very best.

While at the University of Michigan, Clarence studied agriculture as well as math and engineering. He took what he had learned and applied it to the management of his farmland. He was one of the first proponents of erosion control and crop rotation, and these initiatives became the foundation for many modern agricultural practices. Not only did he buy the very best farms, but he created more productive soils with higher rates of fertility. The result was the creation of more valuable lands. He was also known for maintaining his farmland. When he became the owner of a new farm, he cleaned up anything that needed it, built new fence, and repaired barns and outbuildings.[9]

LeBus had already bought several small farms when in 1893, his father Lewis took his family and moved to Los Angeles. At that time, Lewis was the largest land-owner in

Harrison County. He had acquired over 2,000 acres of the best land. When he left for California, he left his two oldest sons back in Cynthiana to manage his farms. They became the virtual owners: what the farms produced was theirs. Clarence and Orie shared in the responsibilities and the profits from this farmland.[10]

On November 5, 1896 at the age of thirty-four, Clarence LeBus married Mary Frazer also of Cynthiana, Kentucky. She was the daughter of Doctor Noah Frazer.[11] The family of Noah Frazer was without doubt one of the more prominent families in the area. Noah Frazer was a large landowner himself. He owned the very fine 400 acre farm that touched the Northeast corner of Cynthiana. Of course that farm was known as the Frazer farm, and it had both a summer home on the hill above town and a city home on what is now Pine Street in Cynthiana. The Union Army encampment during the Civil War (known as Camp Frazer) was on his farmland where it joined the Falmouth Pike. The Frazer Farm later became known by its most recent name of the Handy Farm. Eventually, Clarence LeBus became the owner of the Handy/Frazer Farm.

A year later, Mary and Clarence's first son, Frazer Dunlap LeBus was born. Marriage and fatherhood didn't slow LeBus down. He continued his land purchases, and by 1897 he owned over 2,000 acres of the best farmland.[12] There was in the late 1880s and 1890s very short lived periods of economic growth followed by periods of economic contraction (panics).[13] At this time in his life LeBus timed his land purchases to coincide with the price fluctuations. His farms were used primarily for grazing. Sheep, cattle, horse, hogs and mules were all grazing in his fields. Early on the most prevalent animals grazing the LeBus farmland were mules. There were no tractors at the time, and mules were the primary source of power for the farmers. LeBus sold the mules all over the country. He was a major producer of workhorses as well. But Clarence LeBus by no means took a step away from his interests in tobacco. Of his 2,000 acres, 500 were dedicated to the production of burley tobacco. His yield would have been somewhere in the area of 500,000 pounds of tobacco each year. It is likely that

LeBus had about fifteen different tenant farmers engaged at this time.

The ten years between 1897 and Clarence LeBus's joining the Burley Tobacco Society in 1907 saw significant growth in his business acumen, and he was becoming increasingly better known and more highly regarded. He began to branch out and drift towards enterprises other than tobacco and farming. And once again, as his income continued to increase, he stuck with his practice of buying more farmland. His economic/farming plan became self-fulfilling and his wealth growth was huge.

Four of Clarence LeBus's earliest and most significant business ventures during the ten year period were destined to be very profitable. A bank, pork packing company, stock yards, and an iron fence company were some of his first investment initiatives other than farmland.

It was in October of 1901 that LeBus organized The Harrison Deposit Bank in Cynthiana. LeBus was the primary investor and majority owner, but he refused to be bank president or take any position that required him to work daily in an office other than his own.[14] It was in 1905 that LeBus organized the Union Bank and Trust Company of Lexington, Kentucky.[15] The Stockyards Bank of Cincinnati, Ohio (which subsequently became the Central Trust Company), and the United Bank of Louisville, Kentucky followed.[16] Ultimately Clarence LeBus was a director and owner (or part owner) of eight banks. In addition to the four banks located in Cynthiana, Louisville, Lexington and Cincinnati, he was vested in the People's Bank of Frankfort, Kentucky and smaller banks in the Ohio towns of Cleaves, Clarksville, and Spring Valley.

Being in the banking business didn't slow down Clarence's business of buying and selling tobacco. He left the employ of Bodmann in 1900, and from that point on he was buying exclusively for himself. In the years between 1900 and 1907 hardly a week passed that Clarence LeBus wasn't reported in some small town Kentucky newspaper for having either bought or sold tobacco for record prices. A few random examples are shown here:

> *The Evening Bulletin, Maysville, Kentucky, Jan. 7, 1901.*
>
> J.W. Bentley of Robertson County, has sold his crop of tobacco to Clarence LeBus at 9 cents all around. LeBus paid 8 cents for another crop in Harrison County.

> *The Evening Bulletin, Maysville, Kentucky, July 21, 1902.*
>
> The most interesting feature of the week's sales was the cigarette cutters and wrappers, and the competition for the choice packages in these types was keen, sharp, and lively. Quite a number of them sold from $18.00 to $24.95 per hundred pounds. While four hogsheads of extra fancy bright wrappers sold at $25.25 to $32.00. The latter figure is the record price for the year in the local burley leaf market and was obtained by Clarence LeBus. (sic)

> *The Richmond Climax, Richmond, Kentucky, Sept. 10, 1902.*
>
> A few weeks ago, Clarence LeBus, the well-known tobacco shipper of Cynthiana, Ky., sold a hogshead of fancy burley leaf (cigarette wrappers) in the Cincinnati market at the record breaking price of $46.25 per hundred pounds, a figure that has been equaled but once since the time of high prices during the great Civil War.

> *The Bourbon News, Paris, Kentucky, May 5, 1905.*
>
> Clarence LeBus of Cynthiana, has 1,300,000 pounds of tobacco on hand, of which 500,000 is of his own raising. The past week he bought of Luig and Perkins, of Harrison, 17,000 pounds at 12 cents; of Goodwin and Lizer of Bourbon, 16,000 pounds at 10 cents; of Loui Rhiel of Boubon 10,000 pounds at 9 cents.

> *The Bourbon News, Paris, Kentucky, February 16, 1906*
>
> George Wyatt, of near Paris, sold to Clarence LeBus, of Cynthiana, his crop of 14,000 pounds of tobacco for 10 ½ cents.

> *The Maysville Daily Ledger, Maysville, Kentucky, July 23, 1906.*
>
> Mr. Clarence LeBus of Cynthiana got the record price in ten years on ten hogsheads of tobacco sold last week at the Planters Leaf Tobacco Warehouse in Cincinnati. They were put up by R.Y. Spalding, and brought from $10 to $30.25, one hogshead bringing $368.75.

It's interesting that Clarence LeBus was so successful in his tobacco trading initiatives at exactly the time when there was essentially only one buyer of burley tobacco (The American Tobacco Company.) An interesting view of LeBus and the everyday interaction on the market can be gained from:

> *The Bourbon News, Paris, Kentucky, December 22, 1904.*
>
> ### Clarence LeBus Bluff's the Combine (sic)
>
> Considerable amusement was caused on the leaf tobacco "breaks" Friday at Cincinnati through a challenge thrown down to Colonel Frank Harping, chief buyer of The Continental Tobacco Company (American Tobacco) by Clarence LeBus of Cynthiana, a well-known Kentucky packer and shipper of leaf tobacco.
>
> Mr. LeBus had paid the unusual price of 15 cents per pound for a "crop-lot" of choice leaf tobacco, probably the highest figure in many years for a transaction of this kind. The matter was being discussed on "the breaks." Colonel Harping and LeBus were both present, and Colonel Harping good-naturedly twitted Mr. LeBus on what he considered his lack of judgment as to the present and future values of the weed. (sic)

Quick as a flash LeBus got back at him with an offer to pay him 16 cents per pound for all he could produce of the same quality of goods. Colonel Harping wilted, and declined the challenge amid the roars of laughter of the assembled shippers and manufacturers.

To the uninitiated in the trade it may be said that the point of the story lies in the fact that the combine, with its unlimited millions, was squarely bluff as to the price value by an individual packer. Mr. LeBus is said to have cleared $200,000 in the "whirl" given the market by the Consolidated Company last summer. (The buying power of $200,000 in 1904 equates to approximately $6,000,000 in today's values.)

In the spring of 1904 Mr. LeBus baffled the American Tobacco Company (the trust) with his characteristic business acumen and his endless energy. The trust made LeBus an offer for his 762,000 pounds of tobacco, and LeBus accepted the offer with an option of one week to fulfill the contract. The offer was higher than people with knowledge would have imagined, and LeBus guessed correctly that the Trust was trying to buy the larger holdings of the big players in an effort to corner the market. Seeing the opportunities in the situation, he set out to buy all of the burley tobacco in his area that was still in the hands of the growers before the option expired. By riding constantly and keeping others at work, he bought by the end of the week 440,000 pounds of leaf. On the last night of the week, he rode until eleven o'clock and broke down three horses between two in the afternoon and eleven at night. This tobacco, that otherwise would have been a victim of the corner, he sold to independent factories in Louisville, Detroit, New York and Richmond. It is said he realized a profit of $25,000 for his weeks work ($730,000 at today' value).[17]

The farmer and tobacco merchant began to branch out in the early 1900s. In addition to the Harrison Deposit Bank, he became involved in numerous other small businesses. Mostly they were tobacco and farm related. However, in 1905 Mr. LeBus embarked on two significant business ventures that were stand-alone enterprises. In January of 1905, he opened a pork processing plant in Cynthiana that grew to provide a large number of jobs in the area.[18] The plant was the first factory in the city. During the same month Clarence joined with his brother, Orie, to incorporate the Cincinnati Iron Fence Company. Both of these early ventures proved profitable, and the iron fence company particularly became a significant and very profitable business that remained in the family for over forty years.[19]

* * *

It was also during the year of 1905 that Clarence's father, Lewis LeBus, died in Los Angeles. He had been thrown from a buggy and died from his injuries. Lewis LeBus had not lost his knack for making money after he moved to California in 1893. A particularly intriguing and revealing article appeared in the Los Angeles Herald concerning his estate.

The Los Angeles Herald, Los Angeles, California, Nov. 17, 1905.

LOANS TO FRIENDS, $362,000
Estate of Lewis Lebus in a Peculiar Position

Petition for letters of administration for one of the most peculiar estates in the history of California probate courts was filed yesterday in the county clerk's office by Mrs. Martha C. Lebus widow of the late Lewis Lebus.

The chief item mentioned in the summary of the property is $362,000 money loaned out. Lebus was known among California merchants as one of the most kind hearted of businessmen but it was never imagined that his loans to his friends amounted to such an amount as stated in the petition for probate.(sic)

The entire California estate amounts to nearly $500,000 and Lebus left another large estate in Kentucky. The value of the eastern estate has not been estimated by the heirs.

Other items mentioned in the estate are $17,800 real property. Cash in bank, $13,000; 120 shares of The Los Angeles National Bank $24,000, and 50 shares of the Title Insurance and Trust Company's stock. (Sic)

It is interesting to note that Lewis Lebus had not changed the original spelling of the Lebus name. It would be his sons Clarence and Orie who made the decision to capitalize the "B" in LeBus.

Also noteworthy is that the value today of the $500,000 stated in the petition in 1905 would be over $14,000,000.

* * *

Of course Clarence LeBus continued to add to his central Kentucky land holdings in the ten years prior to his joining the Burley Tobacco Society. He increased his farmland ownership from 2,000 acres in 1897 to 7,000 acres by 1907. Every four or five months during this period, there would be an announcement in some small local paper that Clarence LeBus had bought another farm. The 7,000 acres includes the approximately 1,000 acres that he inherited when his father died. Mr. LeBus didn't waver from his commitment to using whatever money he earned from wherever he earned it to buy more farmland.

The stately A-Keller Home of Lewis LeBus

The A-Keller Distillery joining the A-Keller farm.

CHAPTER SIX

From the Lexington Herald, Lexington, KY, April 26, 1907

Among the principal speakers of the day was Congressman A.O.Stanley, whose discussions of the question at issue, convinced his hearers of his thorough knowledge of the situation: he said:

The enemies of the organization among the farmers have one stock argument which they flippantly prate on all occasions with an air of perfect wisdom and supercilious disdain for the poor benighted hayseed whose stupidity is proof against even their learning and logic.

It is claimed that the small price paid in 1902 and 1903 was due to over production, and that alone.

A close investigation of the conditions prevailing in 1902 and 1903 prove to the certainty of a demonstration that supply and demand had nothing whatsoever to do with the confiscation of the tobacco crop of Kentucky at that time.

Now the price of tobacco in the natural leaf is cut in half, but the price of plug and smoking tobacco, snuff and cigars declines never a cent. The plain truth is, the same sinister power which has destroyed the natural leaf in the hands of the tenant and the farmer has, by its untold outsources and unrestrained powers, maintained at its original cost to the consumer the finished product.

The American Tobacco Company and the American Tobacco Company alone has a direct and pecuniary interest in destroying the price of the raw material (leaf tobacco). To this one Mercedes all-powerful commercial despot, these wretched farmers and producers of tobacco justly attribute all their woes. (Sic)

> From: *On Bended Knees, Billy Cunningham:*
>
> The strangling monopoly of the Duke empire provided the most ruinous blow of all, and by the summer months of 1904, the Duke Trust was a vile curse upon the lips of the tobacco farmers of Kentucky.[1]

It didn't take long. The squeeze was on. The last decade of the nineteenth century saw the buyers of tobacco and the sellers of the crop moving in two different economic directions. The buyers were reduced to only one: The Duke Company became the American Tobacco Company, and that company controlled ninety per cent of the purchases of the white burley tobacco needed for cigarettes. They were making ninety-two per cent of all the cigarettes sold in the United States. The buyers' market belonged almost exclusively to that one company.

The year 1890 marked the high water mark for tobacco in the United States. Everyone from the growers to the buyers, the manufactures and the merchants were making money. In the year 1890, Kentucky tobacco farmers had a bountiful time. Tobacco production increased from just over fifty million pounds to over 220 million pounds. It was then that Kentucky became by far the largest state in the country as measured in tobacco production. There were thirty-eight factories in Kentucky making chewing and smoking tobacco, but none of these were making cigarettes. The largest factories were in Louisville. The largest by far was the National Tobacco Works of Louisville: they were processing about fifteen percent of the total in the United States. For the farmer in the field, prices were settling in at a very profitable eight to twelve cents per pound. The high prices encouraged more production, but that created no real problem as the level of cigarette consumption was growing just as rapidly or even faster.

Until that pivotal date of 1890, competition was fierce in the tobacco business. The number of buyers and manufacturers was huge, and the advertising wars were ferocious. The small farm owners, the big acreage owners and their tenants were all doing well. It was a good time for farming in central Kentucky, and tobacco easily became the main cash crop.

Nationwide, for the most part, farmers were enjoying the longest sustained period of peacetime prosperity that they had ever experienced. But the burley tobacco farmers were starting to miss out on that bounty. As the last decade of the nineteenth century progressed, the capitalistic laws of survival began to prevail. The competing tobacco businesses fell more and more into a smaller number of hands. By the end of the century the small manufacturers had all but disappeared: there was only one significant buyer of white burley tobacco and that was James B. Duke. The Kentucky farmers watched as the price they received for their crop plummeted. In some years during the 1880s the price of burley tobacco reached highs of twelve cents per pound. In 1878, the tobacco in the estate of James Harvey Gray of Harrison County was valued at eight cents per pound, and that was the usual assessment all over central Kentucky.[2] The average price of all burley sold in Kentucky in 1892 was 8.3 cents per pound. That price plummeted to four cents by 1898. By 1902, it was not unusual for a crop to sell for three cents per pound.[3]

The cost of producing burley tobacco in the late 1890s and early 1900s is difficult to determine. The estimates range from five to eight cents per pound. The best-guess consensus settles around six cents per pound. The circumstances were such that, even if he had to sell at less than it cost him to produce the crop, the tobacco farmer really had few options. He was finished with the crop. It was in his hands. He owed money, and his crop was used as collateral. He had to sell, and there was only one buyer.

James Duke's American Tobacco Company was functioning in direct contradiction to the principals and mechanics of a free market economy. The company was engaging in a systematic exploitation and impoverishment of the Kentucky tobacco farmers. A brutal and insidious blow was being delivered to the small farm owners, the tenant farmers, and the families of them all.

The earlier economics of subsistence, gave the farmers hope of surviving hard times. The chief energy sources were the sun and firewood and dependence upon purchased supplies was minimal. But as the cash from a crop of tobacco materialized, the entire rural population became vulnerable to the predation of an economy fundamentally alien to it.[4]

To make things worse, the farmers meanwhile became increasingly more and more sucked into the crop-lean economic system. Since one to two acres of tobacco was all that a single family could tend, the crop lent itself to small plots, and that created the existence of thousands of defenseless independent producers. The tobacco farmers by the nature of their business were vulnerable to exploitation. Those who lived on the land had to have the daily necessities to live from the time the seeds were planted until the crop was harvested a year later. But, they only got paid once a year when the crop was sold. To live, they had to rely on a system of credit, and the local merchants supplied it (with interest of course). At the end of each year, the tobacco farmer had to settle his accounts and retain enough profit to finance the following year's efforts. To catch up, he was always tempted to raise a little more, and usually he did. And often, when he settled up with the merchant, the words that drove thousands of tobacco farmers into poverty and despair were entered following his name: "carried to new book.[5]

Before the 1890s the tobacco farmers could sell their crop in a variety of ways. At many of the general mercantile stores, the crop could be taken directly to the merchant. The merchant would in turn ship the tobacco directly to a major warehouse in Louisville or Cincinnati. Alternatively the farmer could sell his crop to an individual working on his own as a middleman, directly to buyers from one of the local warehouses, or to an agent of the large major warehouses. The farmer could refuse one offer and seek another. However, the American Tobacco Company (ATC/Trust) put an abrupt halt to these options.[6]

The ACT/Trust was the only company buying white burley tobacco, and their methods were simple. In each tobacco producing county, one buyer was assigned to a particular district which was bounded by roads, streams, and other landmarks. The price offer of the buyer was the only one the farmer would receive. If the buyer was unsure of exactly where the farm was in terms of his territory, he would hold off on making an offer until the boundaries could be checked. Of course the prices paid for the tobacco were predetermined by the ATC/Trust, and the whole process was more a matter of procurement and grading than of pricing. If the farmer rejected the offer and later summoned the buyer to return, the second offer was usually less.[7] The Kentucky tobacco farmers were being crushed by a merciless and blind economic force moving in a single direction.

The American Tobacco Company's methods bordered on the sinister. If the crop was small one year the company paid a good price to encourage increased production. If the crop was large, they paid less than the cost of production. By this vicious cycle, they sought to make the country believe that the law of supply and demand was at work, but it was an action that they completely controlled. They were making it all appear to be an outgrowth of the principals of supply and demand in order to cloud the vision of the enforcers of The Sherman Anti-Trust Act. Through cunning and deceit, Duke was able to dodge the Anti-Trust agents until 1911.

For six years, from 1900 through 1906, the state of burley tobacco marketing was locked. It was a tough time for the small farmer. He watched as the price paid for his leaf plummeted. Over the course of the preceding half century he had learned to depend upon his crop for cash, and then there was no cash. It was a period of high emotions. It was a time of despair. The farmer and his family were being crushed by the intensity of the labor and the absence of returns.

From the Lexington Herald, Lexington, KY, Oct. 27, 1911:

> I have seen my father sell the tobacco he has raised to the American Tobacco Company for hardly

the price of the labor put into it. I have seen men and women line up in the fields, a man his wife and his daughter take row for row and work from early morning until night, with the little children asleep in a wagon throughout the dreary day. His children not being educated but made to work for their daily bread. (Sic)

Most of the dialogue and writing has centered on the plight of small Kentucky tobacco farmers, but the large land owners of central Kentucky were getting clobbered as well. While it's sometimes difficult to feel much sympathy for the large farmers with holdings of three hundred acres and more, it is worth noting that they were also distressed. Certainly Clarence LeBus, whose land holdings had grown to over three thousand acres by 1900, and whose primary interest was tobacco farming, was in a difficult place. LeBus and other large landowners were subject to losing everything, and, without doubt, they had more to lose.

The dire situation brought on by the insidious American Tobacco Company monopoly was further exasperated by the mechanics of the tenant farming system on the larger farms. Most of the farms of the north-central Kentucky were less than two hundred acres in size, and their owners raised (as a family) an average of about one and a half acres of tobacco for every one hundred acres of land. These smaller farms relied on the neighbor-helping-neighbor method of meeting the work demands at critical times during the growing season. However the larger land owners relied on tenants to meet the labor demands.

The system of tenant farming in Kentucky was complicated in 1900. The terms as to what the tenant and the landowner agreed to could vary a lot from farm to farm, but there was usually these underlying principles. The tenant was to raise an acre or two of tobacco, and the landowner provided a house for the tenant and his family. The tenant provided the labor (including mules or work horses), and the owner provided the fertilizer. A garden space and a chicken coop were provided by the landowner. The tenant was responsible for his own chickens. One or two meat hogs were to be given to the tenant at hog killing time in late fall, and the tenants all worked at that day-long job. When the tobacco sold, they split the proceeds fifty/fifty.

In addition to these basic agreements, other responsibilities and compensations were often added. There were cattle and hogs to feed, fences to repair, barns and outbuildings were always needing work, and the list around the farms goes on and on. The compensation given to the tenants that did provide extra labor could be as little as twenty five cents to as much as one dollar per day. According to the U.S. Bureau of Labor Statistics, that would equate to between eight dollars and thirty dollars in today's values. The contracts and agreements between the large landowners and their tenants were widely divaricating. There were no set rules. Some tenants did very little work other than raising the tobacco, and others who worked for very large landowners might have raised no tobacco but provided labor wherever it was needed.

It should be noted that, without doubt, today's equivalent of eight dollars to thirty dollars per day seems like very little, and it was. But it was a different time, and the expectations of that time and today were dissimilar. Tenant farmers in 1890s Kentucky lived on the very edge of poverty. They owned no land or home. They raised most of the food they ate. Eggs, corn bread, pork, and home-canned vegetables were there in times of plenty, but of course there was not always plenty. There were no electric bills or water bills. Their small houses were heated with wood. There were no cellphones, cars, health insurance premiums, computers, telephones, natural gas bills, air conditioners or indoor toilets. Most tenant farmers of the late 1890s perceived their needs to be salt, kerosene, sugar, shoes, nails, tools, over-the-counter medicines, and food they couldn't raise.

The Kentucky tenant farmer absolutely had to have the money he received from the sale of his half of the crop. The average tobacco yield in 1900 was somewhere around 1,000 pounds per acre. When the tenant received 10 cents per pound for the crop, his part on 1 1/2 acres was about seventy-five dollars. That would equate to about $2,175 at today's value and that was enough to sustain his meager lifestyle. But when the price dropped to four cents and that amount dropped to $870, he and his family were faced with hunger and devastation.

The tenants were mostly uneducated, and they were poor. They had very little chance of ever improving their conditions or their status. For the most part, every aspect of their life was in the hands of a landowner. With the demise of reasonable tobacco prices, the tenants were faced with a poverty so severe that some were on the brink of loss of life itself. There was no cash for those basics of medicine, flour, sugar, clothing, matches, soap, etc.

In the year 1907, Clarence LeBus owned about 7,000 acres in four central Kentucky counties. He was one of the largest landowners in the area, and his farmland was considered to be the very best. Most of his north-central farms had huge river bottoms, and those that didn't were of mostly level-to-rolling terrain.

The labor requirements were somewhere in the area of one tenant for every one hundred acres (and that would not be high). With his having owned about 7,000 acres, it's easy to see that Clarence LeBus would have had a lot of tenant families living on his farmland. It's impossible to know exactly how many. Of course these relationships were never without hitches, and the everyday dealings were complex and endless.

The relationship between the landowners and their tenants was symbiotic: the mere survival of one was positively dependent upon the survival of the other. This dependence of one upon the other often clouded the complex nature of the motives for just how one regarded the other. The landowner's concern for survival sometimes came across as devotion, while the tenant's concern for survival often came across as loyalty.

Without doubt, the more land the large owners owned, the more dependent they were on the tenants. (The labor requirements to farm 7,000 acres was certainly considerably more than one man could handle). The ATC/Trust monopoly forced tobacco prices so low that everyone in the business was threatened: the tenants with starvation and the large landowners with economic ruin.

The threat to Clarence LeBus's farming interests was great. His annual tobacco crop from farming was about 100,000 pounds per year, and the tobacco that he had purchased from others sometimes approached 1,000,000 pounds. Small landowning farmers were a vital part of his tobacco dealings, and they were hurting. His tenants were the backbone of his farm enterprises and they were in despair. His fortunes depended upon the well-being of these farmers, and as he gradually became increasingly more involved in the organization of the burley tobacco-growers union, he became perceived as a strong supporter of, and advocate for, the rights of the "little man".

Appeals were made to James Duke himself in efforts to get some kind of relief for the tobacco farmer. Duke was not interested. No amount of appeal mattered. Duke would not budge.

James B. Duke was, without doubt, a celebrated man in his day. He was rich and powerful, and men of that ilk were mostly met with adulation. When wealth is the yardstick, underlying values get hazy. Judgment becomes centered on the wealth and only the wealth. Character, and lack thereof, can be obscured by one's ability to make a dollar.

From Vanderbilt to Rockefeller to James Duke, we see confirmation that many of those who achieved great wealth, were often able to do so, not because they were better or smarter but because they were willing to engage in practices that were vicious and exploitative. To them, people were to be used for financial gain. Gaining an upper hand was the objective from the onset. Monopoly was the crowning goal. These men have been celebrated for their financial conquests rather than condemned for their obsession with money.

To be sure, there were many humane and generous people of wealth during the late 19th and early twentieth centuries who were sympathetic to the struggles of the less fortunate. But, if the Kentucky tobacco farmers of the early twentieth century were asked, they would have emphatically said that James B. Duke did not qualify.

For the population in the burley tobacco-raising country, the squeeze was on and they were all feeling the pain. The current status quo could not continue. Economic ruin and starvation were the eminent threats, and it was then, in the late nineteenth and early twentieth centuries, that the threat became too much, and the movement started that organized and empowered the little guy in his fight against the ruthless giant. The solidarity that followed was reflected in one of the most extraordinary insurgent episodes in American history.[8]

Lady in field, worming tobacco plants

CHAPTER SEVEN

The average price of tobacco in Kentucky dropped from eight cents per pound to just over three cents from the 1890s to the early 1900s. Tobacco was the cash crop, and the merchants who provided the necessities also suffered as well as the farmers. The banks too were being crippled. Everybody in the farming community was feeling the strain, but none were as devastated as the small tenant farmer. The entire infrastructure and way of life was geared to the production of tobacco. Ultimately they were working for about twenty cents per day, and the labor was anything but fun. It was grueling work.

> *From The Register of The Kentucky Historical Society, 89, 1991: 266-88. Quoting Kate Strand.*
>
> I don't suppose the Lord ever permitted a harder, hotter, dirtier, filthier, and more nauseating work than that of worming tobacco. . . I have seen my husband at the close of the day take off his overalls and stand them alone, so stiff they would be with tobacco juice. Worming tobacco is bad enough for men, but when women and children have to engage in it human torture reaches its climax. My children have toddled along through tobacco rows at my side crying with pain as their eyes were filled with tobacco juice shot into them by tobacco worms.[1] Sic

People of Kentucky became restless. There were murmurings. Ideas were being proposed: discussions began. Steps towards finding solutions were just ahead. One early spokesman said, "The sleeping lion will be aroused and the American people will yet be delivered from their present slavery to the people whose dishonest dollars now dominate."[2](Sic)

Two movements to combat the devastating circumstances began almost simultaneously, but they were not connected and there was little or no coordination between the two. Their ideas, thoughts, plans, and organizing efforts evolved independently of each other. The very dark tobacco grown in western Kentucky and Tennessee had pretty much settled into certain sections that became known as the Black Patch. That dark tobacco was used exclusively for plug and chewing tobacco. The light colored burley grown in central Kentucky was, on the other hand, used almost solely for cigarette production. The Black Patch farmers organized themselves to combat the Duke trust in one way, and the burley farmers of central Kentucky organized themselves in a distinctly different manner. The two movements eventually led to what became known as the Kentucky Tobacco Wars.

Typically, when one recalls the events of the tobacco growers' movement against James Duke and the American Tobacco Company, they think of western Kentucky, the Black Patch Wars, night riders, the Ku Klux Klan, burning tobacco warehouses, and other forms of extreme violence. What is often lost in history is the story of the burley tobacco movement that was taking place in central Kentucky. The Dark Patch wars in western Kentucky and Tennessee were ridden with fury, while the burley movement was mostly violence free. The Dark Patch insurgency was making headlines while the burley organization was making pragmatic decisions. There were other significant differences in the conditions of the dark tobacco marketplace, the organizational philosophies, the tactics, and the leadership; but, they both shared the motive of defeating James Duke and his monopoly.

While the Black Patch wars are not central to this book, it is of some value to review just what happened there. Of course there had been earlier thoughts and tentative plans, but the significant date that marks the beginning of the movement was September 24, 1904. It was on that day that a meeting was held in Guthrie, Kentucky. Over 5,000 farmers showed up at the tiny town in Caldwell County, Kentucky. The principal players in the organization efforts were, Doctor David Amoss, Guy Dunning, Felix Ewing, and Charles Fort. All four men were educated and farmed tobacco on a large scale.

As early as 1893, Felix Ewing had conceived a plan as he watched the tobacco marketing conditions deteriorate. He reasoned that since the American Tobacco Company monopolized the buying market through consolidation, it seemed reasonable that the farmers could just as easily monopolize the supply. The tobacco farmers would agree universally to pool their tobacco and hold it off the market. The conglomerate would then be forced to raise its prices. This became the mantra for the Dark Patch organization. (And the burley movement as well). Ewing sent out the word to all farmers to meet at Guthrie, and the movement started into motion.

The Dark Tobacco District Planters' Protection Association of Kentucky and Tennessee came into being. Charles Fort was named President. Paper and pencils were passed out, and lines formed to enlist those who would join the pool.

As time passed, many of the rank and file farmers anticipated instant success after the show of force and rattling of swords in Guthrie. They became disgruntled as the ATC/Trust showed no indication of relenting. Perhaps most foreboding was the number of farmers who showed little interest in the Association and refused to join. This became the looming problem: what to do about those who wouldn't join.

Of course the Association knew from the beginning that the ACT/Trustrust would immediately raise the prices paid to those who refused to join the pooling effort, and that presented a serious hurdle. The initial means used to encourage everyone to join were logic, discussion, and persuasion. Unfortunately when these methods didn't work, violence became the motivating method.[3]

Meanwhile, the ACT/Trust wasn't fazed. In addition to

the farmer's reluctance to join the Association, the ACT/Trust had another huge advantage: The dark tobacco could be, and was, raised in other places. It was just through a matter of convenience and ugliness that they even so much as toyed with the Dark Patch growers. Regarding his supply of dark tobacco, James Duke said he had plenty.

In short order the tactics of the Planters Association turned to violence. Groups wearing masks began to ride out on horseback and threaten the farmers who refused to join. At first they would tell their families that they were going hunting, and they thus became known as the "Possum Hunters." Meanwhile, almost simultaneously with the first meetings of the Possum Hunters, David Amoss made an important trip to Nashville Tennessee. There he met with the local Klavern of the Ku Klux Klan. He wanted to know about their organization, rituals, management, and mode of operation. Amoss used this information to organize and recruit men to join a secret society that's sole function was to spread terror to those refusing to join his association, and with this, the Possum Hunters became the Night Riders.[4] It was the history of the Klan in the area that easily lent itself to the violence of the nights.

The early raids of the Night Riders involved mostly "scraping" the seed beds of the holdouts. The beds were destroyed so that the farmers could not set out their crops. When this tactic didn't work, because the farmer just got more plants from others, increasingly more and more violent methods were used. Men were called out of their homes at night and threatened. The masked riders resorted to whipping men in front of their families. Houses and barns were burned. Men were shot and killed.

Towards the end of the duration of the Dark Patch movement, frustration led to more extreme violence: An American Tobacco Company warehouse in Princeton, Kentucky was burned, and on January 4, 1907, the Night Riders torched warehouses in Hopkinsville, Kentucky. That was the event that cemented upon the minds of the American people the images of the Night Riders and their violence.

They became viewed as, and they were, a bunch of ruffians having a grand old time resorting to the practices of the Ku Klux Klan and terrorizing the countryside.

From On Bended Knees, Bill Cunningham, page 76.
Gladys L. Gardner: remembering what she saw as a small child.

"We were living on South Jefferson Street in plain view of the Steger tobacco warehouse two blocks across on Seminary Street when the Night Riders burned that and the Orr tobacco warehouse in the north part of town. It was in the light of that fire that I saw one group of those masked men marching out South Jefferson Street to where their horses were hitched, and ready for their getaway after their job was finished. I was only six years old but I can remember the sound of their boots on that night of November 30, 1906. I was standing at the front door with my mother. We were terrified as the other neighbors were also. My father had walked uptown to near the courthouse, before we understood what it was all about. Several other men who did the same thing got locked up in different places by the Night Riders but no one seemed to notice my father. As the masked men passed our house, they were shooting guns in the air and yelled at us and others to 'get back inside.' The leader of the group raised something to his mouth and blew out three long blasts of indescribable sound, and the Night Riders regrouped and left town indifferent directions."(Sic)

These were years of an agrarian revolution which resulted in useless bloodshed and in a complete upsetting of the state of morale in Kentucky. The Hopkinsville incident and the uncontrolled violence became the crowning blows to the goals of the Planters Association. People on both sides of the issue were fed up. Everybody was living in fear, and the rampant fear led farmers to quit growing tobacco altogether. There was a surge of people who moved out of the state. The prevailing emotion moved from excitement to disgust, and the movement died without accomplishing much at all.

Nevertheless, the Dark Patch movement, and the accompanying Night Riding, brought light to one distinct idea that was also evolving in central Kentucky: the notion of tobacco farmers organizing to oppose the Duke monopoly by holding the harvested tobacco off the market. A result was the birth of the Burley Tobacco Society.[5] While Black Patch organizers struggled in their recruiting effort, the burley cooperative ultimately obtained the backing of almost eighty-five percent of the burley growers in central Kentucky.[6]

As early as May 1898, tobacco farmers in Carroll County, Kentucky met to discuss ways of organizing themselves against the efforts to of the American Tobacco Company and their efforts to establish a "tobacco manufacturing trust" (monopoly). The Carroll County growers resolved only to call on state and federal legislators to enact more stringent anti-trust laws: a move that went nowhere. Meanwhile growers in Bath and Owen counties were mulling over the problem and contemplating what they might do to confront the growth of the Duke trust. Burley tobacco farmers where placed in an ironic position: though the demand for their product was increasing as the cigarette market exploded, the price paid for their leaf continued to fall. The number of cigarettes produced in the United States doubled in just ten years, but while the amount grown increased only slightly, the price paid dropped from 8.5 cents to 5.5 cents.[7]

In July of 1898, burley growers from seven Kentucky counties met and agreed that the ATC/Trust monopoly threatened their farming incomes by, "establishing a degree of servitude more galling and degrading than African slavery or Russian serfdom." The organizer of this meeting was Doctor S.E. Hampers of Carroll County.[8] He began to organize farmers in the burley region to join into a crop withholding organization. His idea was to send representatives to each marketing area, and when they determined that the prices being offered by the ATC/Trust were below the cost of production, they would stop the sale by refusing to put up the tobacco until a fair price was offered. His plan was naive at best, but it was the first that had at its foundation the idea of creating a holdout.

Several other semi-formal meetings were held in other counties around central Kentucky, and other ideas of resistance were brought up. Then in December, 1898 over eighty delegates met in Lexington and selected a title for a new organization: The Kentucky League of Tobacco Growers. W.B. Hawkins was selected to head the committee, and delegates were chosen to organize farmers in their home counties.[9]

The Lexington meeting was significant not only because it was the first serious effort to organize the growers, but also because of the member's universal rejection of one initial proposal. A Woodford County farmer, Tobias Gibson, relayed a plan that he had been advised of that involved harsh controls. In an effort to reduce the total acreage produced, the plan called for every member of the league to be assigned an amount to grow. If an uncooperative farmer intended and tried to grow more that his projected allotment, his tobacco beds would be scraped and destroyed.[10] This was a repeat of the methods used in the Dark Patch region. Gibson's comments stunned the growers, who later publicly rejected the enforcing plan. It was clear from the beginning that the majority of the group wanted no part in violence.

The open and almost universal rejection of a plan that used any violence whatsoever set a foundation that would be quite different from the western Kentucky debacle. The ongoing approach would be based upon unity and organization rather than violence. (Of course, there were isolated incidences of violence, but they were not widespread)

The 1898 Lexington meeting was significant in other important ways: talks and plans began to center around the feasibility of the growers holding their tobacco off the market to force the Duke trust to pay more, and concrete plans were made to inform more farmers of the organization. Also, underlying it all was a plan to build independent warehouses that the members would pay for themselves. Unfortunately, the designers of this plan underestimated just how impoverished the farmers were: Most of the growers were too poor to come up with any cash whatsoever.

The inability to raise money led to the quick demise of The Kentucky League of Tobacco Growers, but it was not all a failure. Some long term positives came from the abrupt failure. While the Growers League did, in fact, prove to be a quick disappointment, it introduced Clarence LeBus and J. Campbell Cantrell to the tobacco movement. Clarence LeBus began to attend any and all organizational meetings, and his name very quickly became universally recognized as a significant player in the development of the movement. From the time of his introduction to the movement, and throughout its infancy, Clarence LeBus attended the meetings and listened: he was not known to be an overly wordy speaker, but when he did speak, people listened. His knowledge of banking, business, and all things related to tobacco gave him a special status.

In 1902 another company was formed: The Farmers' and Growers' Tobacco Association. Representatives from thirty-four Kentucky counties met in Carrollton to write the bylaws, and headquarters were established in Lexington. W.B. Hawkins, the organizer, was named president. Once again, plans called for the pooling of the burley crop and the construction of independent warehouses financed by the farmers, and once again the initiative failed because of the inability to raise money. However, the Growers Association was the first to try the approach of appealing directly to James Duke to try to convince him that the structure of pricing was devastating to the producers. In September, 1903 Hawkins and an associate, W.B. McChord went to New York to see Duke. Of course, Duke was unimpressed. When the McChord offered the pooled 1902 crop to Duke at the price of eight and one-half cents per pound, James Duke blandly responded that he was not in the least bit interested. While he agreed that the farmers had the right to organize, he didn't purchase a single pound of the pooled 1902 crop.

It was becoming obvious to organizers that the idea of any requirement that the farmers themselves had to come up with money wasn't going to work. Several additional attempts to organize the burley farmers took place in late 1902, 1903, and 1904 by Hawkins and McChord. Meetings were held in Lexington and other central Kentucky cities. Appeals were made to banks in New York, Boston, Philadelphia, and Cincinnati, but no money was forthcoming.

Every time that the organizers believed that they were moving towards success, some event doomed their efforts. Perhaps the most devastating negative impact came from the insidious practices of James Duke himself. He refused to bid on any tobacco presented for sale in 1903 by any farmer who had joined the cooperative in 1902. Of course this underhanded practice had the effect of frightening farmers away from joining any future organizing efforts. By 1905, the situation appeared hopeless. The small tobacco farmers were facing ruin as well as starvation.

What the farmers didn't do was give up. The discussions continued and small groups of men and women met frequently. These discussions took place mostly in the communities north of the inner bluegrass area of Kentucky, and the discussions were not limited to only a few meetings. The talks were ongoing and plans were floated everywhere in central and north-central Kentucky. The price and what to do was the topic at the dinner tables and every country store throughout the area. But all the early plans implemented to organize the growers ultimately failed. Between 1898 and 1907, formal meetings were held in most every county seat in the burley district.

Organizers announced that another attempt to organize the farmers to pool their tobacco would begin after the 1906 selling season ended. One event made this effort different than all the others. It was marked by the presence of a national organization that viewed the circumstances of the burley tobacco marketing situation as a test case. That organization wanted to prove itself as a national farmers union that could raise the prices for all agricultural producers. It was known as the American Society of Equity.

The Equity society (as it became known) was created by James A. Everitt of Indianapolis. Everitt was not a farmer but an operator of a feed store and newspaper owner. He had no experience in organizing but seemed genuinely concerned about the plight of the American farmers as they faced the brutality of fixed prices. His organization offered nothing new, but it had the image of a national organization and that was instrumental in getting people together.

In February 1906 growers in New Castle met to hear an explanation of the Equity plan. The result was the formation of the Henry County Union. H.E. Swain was the chief organizer of the new venture. In March 1906 Swain organized local unions in the Henry County communities of Bethlehem, Franklinton, New Castle, and Smithfield. During the spring and summer of 1906, Swain and M.C.Rankin urged farmers throughout the burley district to join a pooling program. The result was the formation of eight county unions. On October 1, 1906 the eight unions of Grant, Henry, Owen, Pendleton, Henry, Spencer, Trimble and Washington counties met in New Castle and formed the latest organizational effort. And thus was born the Burley Tobacco Society. [11]

A meeting with the Commercial Club of Winchester, Kentucky was scheduled in an effort to grow the Society. The group was met with enthusiasm, and the Winchester club agreed to provide stenographers and secretaries. More than 3,500 letters were sent to well-known farmers in the area asking them to attend a crucial tobacco conference to be held in Winchester. When the meeting arrived, an enthusiastic gathering of tobacco farmers decided to launch a coordinated campaign to organize the entire burley region. The subsequent organizing effort was led by H.E.Swain, G.W.McMillen, C.M.Hanna, and M.C.Rankin. A total of twenty organizers went out to cover the entire burley district in a tightly controlled effort to organize the growers.

The growers decided that unless fifty percent of the estimated ninety-two thousand acres of burley grown in the area were pledged by January 1, 1907, the pooling effort would be canceled. The organizing network built by the BTS (Burley Tobacco Society) labored feverishly to recruit during this critical period. On new-year's day, 1907, growers from twenty-nine counties met in Lexington to report on the amount pooled in each county. When the results were tabulated, it was calculated that fifty-four percent of the acreage had been included in the pool, and the county organizers rushed to the telephones to send word back to their individual counties that the goal had been met. Within weeks of the Lexington meeting, the BTS/pool announced that it controlled sixty-five percent of the burley crop. James Everitt and his Equity Society immediately began claiming credit for the success, but in reality they had practically nothing to do with the work, the organization, nor the success. Ultimately almost eighty-five percent of all burley farmers joined and twenty-six Kentucky counties (plus two in Ohio and one from Indiana) were represented.

From his introduction to the movement in 1898 until the creation of the BTS/pool in 1906, Clarence LeBus was totally immersed in the activities, plans, discussions and recruiting efforts of the Society. He spoke at each of the twenty-six counties that ultimately became members in the BTS/pool. His expertise in the tobacco business coupled with his organizational skills and ability to drive himself through long hours of work so impressed the fellow organizers that they considered him to be indispensable to the effort. He was a driving force.

Clarence LeBus was always known as a man of few words, but when he was on the road engaged in the effort to recruit members to a cooperative organization aiming to pool their crops, he became a forceful and powerful orator.

Words from Ernest Helm as printed in the Lexington Herald, Lexington, Kentucky, October 17, 1909.

Mr. LeBus has the reputation for using fewer words per square idea than any (speaker or writer) ever boasted. If he had been called upon to write the constitution, he would have written the word "pool" on a card and handed it to King George and challenged the royal right to dictate to tobacco planters.

> *And also from the Lexington Herald, Lexington, KY, October, 1909.*
>
> On one or two occasions, when large results hung on small developments, I have seen him display a rugged eloquence which was magnetic. The day he swung Bracken County to the pool column in an impromptu speech of two hours, her (the county) joining the pool seemed a certainty.

At the time of the Lexington meeting, Clarence LeBus owned seven thousand acres and was raising over four hundred acres of tobacco. It was at this meeting on January 1, 1907 that Clarence LeBus was elected president of the BTS. The salary that he was to be paid was set at the staggering figure of $25,000 per year. (This amount calculates to about $700,000 at 2020 values). Through his skills, knowledge and work ethic, LeBus had gained an unequaled reputation, and he was considered to be indispensable to the efforts of the Burley Tobacco Society (BTS/pool)

> *Lexington Herald Leader, Lexington, Kentucky, October 17, 1909.*
>
> Type has been worn out with discussion of the "LeBus Salary." It is fair to assume that the District board of the Burley Tobacco Society composed of co-planters from forty five counties got him as cheaply as it could. It is doubtful whether the majority would have offered any five-figure amount if it had been left to them to fix a salary at the onset. But twenty-five thousand dollars was the price demand of the man who refuses to be cheap in anything; and the board regarded him as indispensable. The board has reviewed this valuation at least five times, and five times it has restated its legitimacy.

What followed the appointment of Clarence LeBus to the position of president of the BTS/pool was, without doubt, a brutal struggle between the small guy and big business.

Program of Burley Tobacco Society Banquet, Charence LeBus in center.

*Headline of Clarence LeBus
and James Duke*

CHAPTER EIGHT

Clarence LeBus' involvement in the struggle between the tobacco farmers and James Duke's American Tobacco Company was without doubt of paramount importance to the pooling effort, but there were other factors of major significance as well. The importance and nature of white burley tobacco, the growing conditions in Kentucky, and the work traditions of the small farmers were also vital. Success of the pooling effort would probably have been doomed from the onset without the combination of these factors.

In the late spring of 1868, an incident took place that was profound in terms of its impact upon the history of American agriculture. The strange event took place on a small tobacco farm, and to this day the exact cause has not been explained. George Walsh of Brown County Ohio was in the process of setting out his tobacco beds when he ran out of the tiny seeds. His farm was across the Ohio River from Augusta, Kentucky, and it was there that more seeds could be purchased. He sent two of his helpers to ferry across the river, buy some seeds, and return to the farm to finish with the beds. No problems developed: The plants grew, were set out, and at the end of the summer, the finished product was cut and housed in good order. But there was a noticeable difference in the plants that grew from the Kentucky seeds and all the other seeds previously used. That difference was easy to see from the time the tiny plants first sprouted until the crop was cut and housed. The plants were very light in color, lighter in weight, and lighter in texture.[1] The leaves were larger than what were normally seen, and like the leaves, the stems and stalks were also light in color and weight. It was the first time the tobacco world had seen the light plants. What followed was a strain of tobacco that was later to be called "white tobacco."

George Walsh's handling of the plants was important as well. Either by plan, design, or just accident, the lighter plants had been set out in a field removed from the fields planted with traditional seedlings. What Walsh did know was that he had something new. What he didn't know was whether it was good and had potential, or if it was bad and a waste of time to pursue. What George Walsh did know was that he was going to keep some of the seeds produced by the light tobacco. He planned to set out a field of the new strain far removed from other tobacco so that it couldn't be cross pollinated. And, that is what he did.

This new variety of tobacco soon spread across the Ohio River into the northern counties of Kentucky. In short order, it was discovered that the new strand had an absorptive quality that was far higher than that of any other tobacco type. At that time almost all tobacco grown went to the manufacture of plug/chewing tobacco. Cigarette production was in its infancy. Plug tobacco was made by first indoctrinating cured tobacco with different sugars and syrups and then pressing it into squares. The new white tobacco took up more than twice its weight in the liquids. Its co-efficient of absorption was 2.60 while the absorption co-efficient of the other types was 1.48.[2] If you were to have cut into a sample of plug tobacco made from the earlier dark types, you would have found the gumminess between the leaves and not incorporated throughout the leaf. The new leaf soaked it up. When the absorptive quality of the new white tobacco was discovered, it became a must-have product for the plug tobacco industry.

There seems to be little doubt that David Walsh was in fact the first person to notice the white tobacco, but the story continues with the suggestion that a Mason County farmer named David Burley was instrumental in the introduction and promotion of the new variety. History suggests that Mr. Burley got some of the seeds that Walsh had originally saved and that he began to isolate and cultivate the white type. He began to provide seeds to other Mason County farmers, and eventually, the new variety made its way to the large farms of central Kentucky. It was from him that the tobacco type became known as "burley" tobacco.

In addition to the absorptive value of the burley tobacco, it was soon determined that this new type had a nicotine content of only 2.80 percent as against 5.8 and 6.0 percent of the other known varieties.[3] This too made it valuable for use in plug tobacco, but it did not end there. The impact of the low nicotine in tobacco used for cigarette production was of absolute and unquestioned importance.

Cigarette production exploded after the Civil War. The availability of burley tobacco was in its infancy at about the same time. The first cigarette did not have any burley tobacco in them, and they had a harsh and bitter taste. When, for whatever reason, some burley was purchased on the markets by the cigarette makers, and added into the blend, it was discovered that cigarettes made with the new white tobacco had not only a better taste but were much milder as well. Soon, that was all the smokers wanted. It became apparent early on that burley was absolutely necessary for cigarette production. If the producers wanted to sell cigarettes, they had to have the new white tobacco.

The extraordinary abilities of Clarence LeBus coupled with the reality that burley tobacco was absolutely necessary to the manufacture of cigarettes were two powerful advantages for the farmers in their movement to hold out the crops until they received higher prices. But there was a third, and equally important, ingredient to the power of the cause. Burley tobacco could only be grown effectively in central Kentucky: weather and soil were the principal players in this phenomenon.

It was believed at the time that the limestone based soil of Kentucky was needed for burley production. While this theory has been largely debunked, it is important to know that it was an unchallenged belief at the time. What cannot be challenged is the fact that the weather patterns of Kentucky provided conditions that were found nowhere else, and these conditions were absolutely necessary for the curing of burley tobacco.

When the burley tobacco was cut in the field at the end of the growing season, each plant was speared on a tobacco stick. Five or more plants were affixed to each stick. After being left in the field to soak up the sun for two or three days, the tobacco was loaded on a wagon and hauled to a barn. The sticks of tobacco were hung between rails where they were left to "cure" for eight to twelve weeks. It was (and still is) in this curing process that the magic of Kentucky weather comes in to play. A long growing season, hot dry days, and cooler moist nights allowed the tobacco to transform into a state that was absolutely necessary for cigarette production.

After the green tobacco is hung in the barns, the green leaves start to dry and turn into a light brown color. When the leaves are dry and the weather is hot, they become very brittle. When the humidity level is up, a condition known by the tobacco farmers as "in case" takes place. The tobacco is said to be "in case." This means that the leaves have absorbed enough moisture to make them soft and pliable. The leaves transform from a condition somewhat like a dry cracker to a pliable condition somewhat like thin leather.

The process of going "in case" and then back "out of case" is absolutely necessary for production of cigarette tobacco, and it has to take place many times during the curing season. Kentucky weather provides the conditions for this action to take place. It was only in Kentucky that the conditions were perfect for burley tobacco: a long growing season, hot days, and humid nights.

The importance of this Kentucky weather to the initiative of holding tobacco off the market in an effort to force James Duke to increase the price he was paying for the crops was a huge factor. It was well known that Duke had millions of pounds of the burley tobacco stored and on hand for use. Of course, he would continue to use this inventory as long as it would last. What he couldn't do was just go somewhere else and raise the crop. If he could have, certainly he would have. But the uniqueness of Kentucky weather stood in his way.

A fourth and equally important circumstance favoring the farmers in their war against the brutal monopoly initiated by the American Tobacco Company was, quite simply, the manner in which the crop was raised. The culture of close-knit neighbors sharing work and equipment was established when the small hill farms were first settled. Very rarely was a crop of burley tobacco raised by a single family without the help of neighbors. Raising a tobacco crop was an exceptionally labor intensive endeavor.

During the early summer plant setting time it was the usual procedure for neighbors to help neighbors. But when cutting and housing began, the labor requirements multiplied. Day after day, small groups of neighbors rotated from farm to farm depending upon the readiness of each crop. Some might be cutting and spearing the crop on one farm, while others could be loading wagons on another. Later in the day they might all meet up together to house the crop in the barn. The men and women invariably worked well together: It was necessary and imperative for their survival.

The result of this "neighboring" was the development of thousands of tiny close-knit communities. A trusting population evolved. Neighbors moved freely from farm to farm. Tools were borrowed, ponds fished, and coons hunted. Permission had been granted years in the past, and it was understood. The land of others was treated as land of yours.

This community mindset was an important factor in the organizational effort. The farmers trusted each other. As the movement spread, an almost club-like allegiance transpired. It was easy for the small farmers to buy into the feeling that they were all in it together. Organizing the independent minded is, at best, difficult, but with these farmers it was different: Once a core group bought onto the effort to pool the tobacco, the word spread and confidence prevailed.

There had been attempts to organize the American farmers prior to the tobacco wars of 1906-1909. None had been particularly successful. The four powerful forces that the BTS/Pool had working in its favor cannot be stressed too much. The unique nature of the plant itself, and its necessity for acceptable cigarettes, coupled with the fact that burley could only be grown in Kentucky, put the American Tobacco Company at a disadvantage from the onset. Thirdly, the club-like mentality of the small Kentucky farmers was a powerful positive.

CHAPTER NINE

> *From The Louisville Times, November 30, 1907:*
>
> The American Tobacco Company is generally considered to be one of the most typical of America's monopolies or trusts. It was incorporated in New Jersey on October 19, 1904. It merged and took over the assets of the American, Continental, and Consolidated Tobacco Companies at that time. Nearly every man who got in on the ground floor is now a millionaire. It has a surplus of $32,440,193 and last year paid out $5,000,000 in dividends on its preferred stock, over $10,000,000 on its common, and placed nearly $7,000,000 in the surplus fund.[1] (Sic)

> *And from The Louisville Times, November 30, 1907:*
>
> One who has devoted considerable time in an effort to ascertain the exact amount of tobacco which the trust has on hand said, "No one knows this but the Lord and President Duke."[2] (Sic)

James Duke was not worried. Of course he knew of every move the growers were making, but he was sure of himself, and he was convinced that the poor ignorant hillbilly tobacco farmers would fail in their efforts to organize. Even if they did get some kind of movement going, they would never be able to keep it going, and they would never survive his maneuvers.

Years before the January, 1907 organizing of the Burley Tobacco Society (BTS/ pool), James Duke introduced one of his cutthroat practices by taking advantage of the prevailing tobacco marketing system to make sure that he could always buy tobacco at a low price. The farmers were handicapped by a weak marketing position. Their basic inability to adjust supply to demand created a chronic tendency to overproduce. Good prices always led to overproduction the next year. When prices fell, however, there was not necessarily an equivalent cutback in production. Farmers generally responded to lower prices by increasing production in an effort to minimize losses. Duke was certainly aware of this vulnerability, and he moved to take advantage of it by maintaining a three year supply. This assured that he never had to pay a high price for the tobacco produced: If in any year the crop was short, pushing prices up, they did not have to buy at the higher prices. He could afford to wait. The growers could not.[3]

When stories of the farmers' talks about organizing to keep the tobacco off the market began to drift into his offices, Duke upped the ante. He realized immediately that having huge amounts of the burley in his hands would work to his advantage in combating any effort by the farmers to control the supply. By mid-1905 he was buying (at low prices) and storing all he could get, and he kept secret his intentions as well as the amounts he owned. Nobody except those closest to Duke knew just how much of the leaf he actually owned. To this day, no one really knows.

Perhaps Duke's most insidious intent was to use the same strategy he used in 1902-1903 to influence the outcome. It was then that he refused to bid on any tobacco presented for sale in 1903 by any farmer who had joined the pool in 1902. Of course this underhanded practice had the effect of frightening farmers away from joining any future organizing effort. By 1906, and the organizing of the BTS/pool, the situation appeared hopeless. Organizing against Duke would prove to be no simple matter.[4]

Duke knew, of course, that a large number of farmers would not sign up for the (BTS/ Pool) and join the effort to pool the 1906 crop. He was shocked to hear that the first sign-up ended with fifty-four percent participation. Within two weeks that figure jumped to sixty-five percent. Those who signed on knew full well that Duke's intimidating practices of 1902 and 1903 would be repeated. There was a deep sense of urgency all around.

January 1, 1907 was the first day of existence for the BTS/pool, and it was on that same day that Duke sent his agents into action. Their message to all burley producers was clear: American Tobacco Company (ATC/trust) would significantly increase the amount paid for tobacco produced by non-members of the pool but would never bid on tobacco produced by those involved in any way in the pooling effort. If the movement failed and Duke prevailed, participants in the pool would be put out of the tobacco business for life.

Duke's control of cigarette production enabled him to operate from a position of great strength, but there was more. Not only did he control the mechanisms for marketing, but he was not above threats, coercion, and other questionable, and even illegal, practices. From the onset, it seemed to uninvolved observers that the chances for success of the BTC/pool were slim to none. Historically, movements to organize the farmers had started off with great enthusiasm (and they still do), but when results weren't immediate, money got short, and lifestyle disruption loomed, the membership corroded quickly.

So the stage was set. On the one hand there was James Duke and his ATC/trust, and on the other was Clarence LeBus and the organization of the BTS/pool. It was certain that Duke was not going to yield to the appeals of the burley growers to raise prices, and it was equally obvious that the pool was to be led by a man, Clarence LeBus, who didn't accept failure as an option in anything that he undertook. Both men were sure of themselves. The situation was at an impass.

———◆———

In October, 1905, fourteen months before Clarence Lebus was elected to lead the BTS/pool, he went to New York to meet with James Duke. Of course his efforts led to nothing. A month later in November, 1905, Lebus again took to the rails. Mr. LeBus went to Washington, D.C. to engage Senator Elkins of West Virginia and Senator Clark of Montana in an effort to encourage them to establish a program that would pay the farmers a better price than the trust was paying and hold the tobacco off the market until James Duke was forced to pay more. There seemed to be reason to believe that something would come of the project until Senator Elkins became sick with a protracted illness.

On his way by train back to Kentucky Clarence LeBus had plenty of time to think. It was during this trip that he formed a plan to combat the Duke monopoly. Upon his return, he approached some of the largest tobacco producers with the idea that if fifty large land owners joined together and started a cigarette manufacturing company they could eliminate the middle man and sell their product directly to the consumer. At first it seemed as if the plan was getting some serious consideration, but inherent difficulties led to its demise. Many of the potential investors were reluctant because they believed that the project would take too long and give Duke the time to devise plans to defeat the initiative. It seemed to a majority of the people close to the circumstances that the time was right to organize all of the growers, and the factory plan could create a delay that would destroy that dynamic. There were others who thought that the factory idea merely shifted the competitive nightmare to a different level and did little to actually eliminate Duke's monopoly. These factors coupled with the difficulties of financing led LeBus to abandon the notion while it was still in its infancy.[5]

It is notable that the two trips that Clarence LeBus took, first to New York and then to the city of Washington, took place more than a year before he was named president of the

BTS/pool. Shortly after his introduction into the movement in 1898 he began to attend meetings and discussions mostly in his home territory of Harrison, Bracken, Grant, and Robertson Counties. By 1900 LeBus was involved in all formal discussions wherever they were taking place. He was soon considered indispensable. By the time of his two trips, Clarence LeBus had assumed hypothetical ownership of the burly pooling efforts. After the unsuccessful meetings, and the subsequent demise of the fifty-grower plan, the discussions turned exclusively to the best way to create a strategy that would allow the growers to keep the tobacco off the market until Duke was forced to buy.

It appears from most everything written about the character of Clarence LeBus that he was a man of kind, caring, and generous qualities. Assuredly, he had the interests of all of the tobacco growers from the poorest tenant farmer to the wealthiest Kentucky land owner as his primary motivation. However it is noteworthy that LeBus had a huge personal interest in the pooling success as well. In May of 1905 he had on hand 1,300,000 pounds of tobacco; 500,000 pounds were from crops of his own raising and 800,000 pounds that he had bought from others. He continued to buy and sell tobacco up until the time that he was named the BTS president.

> *From The Bourbon News, Paris Kentucky, May 5, 1905:*
>
> The past week Clarence LeBus bought of Luig & Perkins, of Harrison County, 17,000 pounds at 12 cents; of Goodwin & Lizer, of Bourbon, 16,000 pounds at 10 cents; of Louis Rheil, 10,000 pounds at 9 cents.[6] (Sic)

In the two to three years immediately preceding the beginning of the BTS/pool in 1907, Clarence LeBus continued to buy tobacco crops at four and five times what the American Tobacco Company was paying for the average crop. The crops were separated into several different grades, and there was some variance within the grades. Certainly the high prices he was paying was for the very best tobacco within the choicest grades. There were a few independent cigarette producers still operating, and it is likely that LeBus believed they would buy what he bought. What is known is that Clarence LeBus continued to buy tobacco at high prices, that he continued to grow tobacco that he did not sell, and that he had a big store of tobacco that he had bought from others.

When he agreed to lead the effort, LeBus refused to commit to pooling the tobacco that he owned before the January, 1907 date of his presidency. LeBus stated to the body of delegates that if pooling his 1904 and 1905 holdings were made a condition of his becoming a member of the society, he could not join it. He gave as his reason that he had already carried the 1904 holding for two years and the 1905 for one year and that he would not obligate himself to carry them indefinitely.[7] The BTS/pool membership readily agreed. LeBus also pledged that throughout the duration of the pooling efforts, he would personally buy no additional tobacco.[8]

The official beginning of the BTS/pool and the naming of LeBus as president came at the right time for both the organization and for the man as well. The farmers needed LeBus and his skill-set, and LeBus would, without doubt, benefit from the power of the people to sell his own tobacco holdings. The time was right:

From The History of Kentucky and Kentuckians, E. Polk Johnson, Lewis Publishing Company, 1912, page 612

> It will thus be seen that Mr. LeBus had felt with special force the heavy hand of the Tobacco Trust and that he had made such efforts as one man could make to cope with its power. But the entire tobacco producing population had felt the same power, and in 1906 there was an almost spontaneous uprising in the hill counties of the Burley Tobacco belt in Kentucky, which spread into the Blue Grass region and into the tobacco growing counties of Indiana, and Ohio. (Sic)

And from the same source, page 611:

> A prominent Cincinnati tobacconist and warehouseman once said of him: LeBus never loses his head nor any of his money.[9] (Sic)

Once again, it seems best to revisit the traits of the communal culture of rural Kentucky. From its onset and throughout its existence, the BTS/pool was empowered by the Kentuckians' concept of neighbor helping neighbor and the sense of kinship that it propagated. A farm family's closest neighbor was usually given a status almost equal to that of "family." Shortly before the official formation of the BTS/pool, a representative from each member-county was appointed. It was planned, and the idea implemented, that this leader would pick additional representatives throughout his county. These men (and a few women) would be chosen for their perceived degree of influence, and they would constitute a county board.

While the degree of influence that these county board members were perceived to possess was certainly an important consideration, it was no more important than the question of where they lived within the boundaries of the county. Where they were was just as important as who they were. By choosing representatives from all areas of each county, their influence would spread like circles until each ring of influence overlapped the others. Each farm family was inclined to join their neighbors. There developed an almost familial sense of belonging. An attitude developed that everyone was in it together. Clarence LeBus and the early organizers were well aware of how this "neighboring" influence could be used and they implemented it to perfection. The support of one for the other became the persistent personality of the BTS/pool.

Unlike the selling trends during the mid and late 1900s, the burly markets in 1900-1910 did not open until sometime in January of the following year. Some tobacco was sold to agents as early as November, but most sales commenced after the first of the year. In those earlier years, the jobs that had to be completed before the tobacco stripping began took a lot longer than in the later years. Planting the cover crops, shucking the corn, killing hogs, and finishing the vegetable canning were all time consuming endeavors. Then, on top of that, October was considered to be, "firewood month." Thus, the first day of 1907 was the appropriate time to begin the organization to deal with the 1906 crop.

Of course, the underlining intent of the pooling effort was to enable the farmers to keep the 1906 crop off the market in order to force James Duke to increase the prices he was paying. It was no secret to anyone that the white burley tobacco was necessary for cigarette production, and that it could only be raised in and around Kentucky. It was the belief of LeBus and the other organizers that these considerations gave the BTS/pool a reasonably strong hand.

Organizing what was to become universally recognized as "the pool" was a somewhat complex undertaking. Millions of pounds of burley tobacco were to be received, weighed, graded, recorded and stored. The logistics and mechanics of how this process was to unfold for the 1906 crop were, for the most part, decided months before the January 1, 1907 organizational date.

The individual crops first had to be weighed and graded upon delivery to the warehouses set up in different counties as receiving "barns." The poundage and grades were recorded in each farmer's name. The tobacco was then to be pressed according to grades into large wooden barrels called hogsheads. One or two men stood in the hogshead while the tobacco was handed to them, and they pressed it down with their feet until it was full to the top. They stepped out and moved to another barrel. This process was known as "green prizing." The hogsheads were then sent to warehouses throughout the region where they were to be stored until a satisfactory price could be obtained. It was believed by most that price relief would occur early in the 1907 selling season and that James Duke would bend to the BTS/pool demands and pay as much as twelve cents per pound for the 1906 crop.

From the beginning, each county had its own organization within the whole of the BTS/pool. It was ultimately decided that each individual county would cover the initial expenses of handling the crop for its members, so the exact figure varied a little from county to county. Generally the warehouses were to get twenty-five cents per hogshead (about 1,200 pounds of tobacco) per month for storage. In addition, they were to receive three dollars per hogshead when the crop was ultimately sold. Insurance was one dollar and thirty-two cents per 100 pounds. The individual farmers did not have to insure their personal crops. The leaders of the BTS/pool assured their members that the total costs would not exceed twenty-five cents per pound. The selling fee of three dollars per hogshead was to be paid to the individuals who had advanced the money whenever the crops ultimately sold.[10]

It is not surprising that the BTS/pool gained the cooperation of the local banks. The leaders of the financial industry believed that the BTS/pool was being overseen by accomplished businessmen. The banks had confidence in the plan. A report by the Firefighters Insurance Underwriters succinctly endorsed the financing of the pooling effort. They believed that the BTS/pool would be successful in its purpose and that it was being led by capable men who had the confidence and public sentiment of the general public.[11] Of course, the support of the banks was also grounded in the place that tobacco occupied in the local economy. Higher tobacco prices would not only alleviate the farmers' plight but would also produce two other effects. Increasing the money in farmers' pockets stimulated consumer demand and thus retail trade. Secondly, an improved tobacco economy also strengthened the loan portfolios of the local bankers. Of course, it should be noted that Clarence LeBus was the owner and director of several banks himself. Certainly his influence was important in the banks' almost universal support, but his bank ownership did, in fact, offer the potential for personal profit from the movement as well. With the pooled tobacco acting as collateral, the bankers hoped to realize a profit of their own from higher prices. This alliance provided a rare moment in American agriculture history: a conjunction of creditors and debtors joined in a common cause.[12]

On January 1, 1907, the plan was put into play, and Clarence LeBus was the undisputed leader, both in theory and in practice. Of course LeBus was well aware that James Duke would do whatever he could to destroy the effort; but he trusted in himself, and he believed that the BTS/pool plan was good. By that time, the organization had the support of seventy-five percent of the burley growers, and those members appeared to be firm in their support. All of the twenty-six counties in the Kentucky burley growing region were members of the BTS/pool. The banking community was supportive, as were most local merchants, and the warehouses and other necessary physical facilities were ready to go. The leadership from top to bottom was exceptional, and the belief of most people involved was that when Duke and his American tobacco Company realized that the amount of burley available was seriously compromised, he would in short time, relent and agree to higher prices.

The opening of the tobacco market in Kentucky was a big deal during nearly all of the twentieth century. The markets had always opened with a bang, but in the spring of 1907 it was almost unnoticeable. Thirty-one thousand farmers had contracted to pool their tobacco, and beginning with the first days of January they had already begun to send their crops to the BTS/pool to be prized (pressed) and stored. In a normal year 180,000,000 pounds of white burley would hit the marketplace. The crops would be sold at the auction warehouses, and privately to agents representing independent producers, and certainly to the American Tobacco Company. However this year was different; there was no auction, and only 43,000,000 pounds of burley produced by the 11,000 farmers who refused to join the pool were available to the buyers.[13]

The BTS/pool members were advanced the five cents per pound when their crops were delivered to the pool for storage, but that was pale when compared to what James Duke and his cronies began to pay to the non-members. The average price paid for all grades of white burley in 1906 for the 1905 crop was a little over six cents per pound. The price offered by

Duke to the non-members was a staggering twelve cents per pound. Duke's agents infiltrated the area and contacted every non-member they could locate (and that ended up being all of them) to make the offer and of course, buy the crops.

Duke believed that any ordinary person would immediately abandon the pool and take the unheard of figure of twelve cents. The twelve cent offer was meant to be a knockout blow to the BTS/pool, but its effect ended up having just the opposite effect: It tended to solidify the members' resolve, and it nurtured a determination to dig in.

Of course LeBus and the other leaders of the BTS/pool knew that Duke would raise the prices paid for the crops of the non-members, but they had no idea by how much. The twelve cent figure was higher than they had anticipated, but it fit perfectly into LeBus's plan. He had intentionally put off announcing the price goal that the BTS/pool would hold out for until after Duke began to pay the non-members for their 1906 crop. As soon as the trust began to buy the crops of those outside of the pool, LeBus immediately notified all BTS/pool members that they were holding out for twelve cents per pound. This was passed along to everyone: members and non-members, the press, everyday citizens, and the agents of The American Tobacco Company. This presented James Duke with a serious ethical, legal, and logical dilemma: He was well aware of the anti-trust laws, and buying from one and not the other would be impossible to explain if that practice continued for an extended period of time. Duke had hoped that the twelve cent figure would immediately crush the pooling effort, but in fact it solidified the belief of the BTS/pool members that James Duke was motivated only by profit motive. Dukes disdain for the Kentuckians who were enabling his wealth was obvious, and the intense hatred that the BTS/pool membership felt towards James Duke intensified. This all added to the sense of loyalty that the members felt towards each other. As hoped by the BTS/pool leadership, the move by Duke to dramatically increase, by such a huge amount, what he would pay for the tobacco of the non-members backfired. James Duke underestimated his adversary and the resolve of the members of the Burley Tobacco Society (BTS/pool).

James Duke was by no means timid in his business practices, and he was fearless in the face of competition. During the spring months of 1907, many overtures were made to Duke and his agents seeking some kind of resolve and a price that both sides could agree to; but the American Tobacco Company leader would not budge. Not only did he refuse to buy a single pound of the 137,000,000 pounds of white burley that the pool had stored, but he repeatedly stated that he wasn't concerned.

In early 1907, the first question asked when one person met another at the country store, the church, or on the roads was, "Any news on the pool?"

The answer was always the same: "Nothing!"

All of the tobacco farmers were focused on any news of a sale, or likelihood of a sale, of the pooled tobacco. But there were no sales. By April 1907, all of the burley had been delivered and stored. It was apparent that Duke and his ATC/trust were not going to buy a single pound of the 1906 crop. The tobacco season had not only become monotonous, but it was disheartening as well.

Clarence LeBus and the leadership of the BTS/pool were faced with a serious twofold challenge. First, they had to focus on what was to be done going forward: The farmers had already prepared to plant their 1907 crops while not a single pound of the 1906 crop had been sold. Secondly there was the potential that the almost universal discouragement would lead to disenchantment. They could not turn back now, not with over 130,000,000 pounds of unsold but collateralized tobacco. It was imperative that the BTS/pool lose none of its members.

It is significant that in the spring of 1907, when the BTS/pool was in its infancy, there was little or no violence directed towards the non-poolers by the BTS/pool membership. Threats to the non-poolers were at a minimum, and the feelings towards them by the BTS/pool membership were more contempt and disrespect than anger. Membership in the pool carried with it a certain pride: It was considered to be the right thing to do. It was the neighborly thing. To the 30,000 members and their families, it was believed to be somewhat shameful to not join the Burley Tobacco Society. This view provided a cementing force to the determination of the BTS/pool membership to stick with their commitment: they did not want to be viewed with the same shame that they reserved for the non-member holdouts. The BTS/pool leadership was well aware of the power of this sentiment, and beginning in mid-spring of 1907, it became somewhat of a veiled theme in their speeches and discussions. Of course, everyone was also well aware of the financial disaster that would ensue if they just hung it up and quit. (It should be noted here that there were incidences of violence later in the campaign.)

Without doubt Clarence LeBus had a commanding way of instilling confidence in those around him. He was certainly a relatively young man, having reached the age of forty-two, but his reputation was huge throughout the region. LeBus was not only known for his staggering farming and business accomplishments, but he was considered smart, very smart. His mastery of mathematics and success at The University of Michigan was impressive at a time when very few citizens were even able to attend school past the first few grades. When he spoke, people listened. Mr. LeBus knew that his challenge in the late spring of 1907 was to keep the BTS/pool membership intact, and he set out to do exactly that. The topics of his speeches and talks took on a new slant: He set out to convince the membership that they were winning the battle with the American Tobacco Company. He exuded confidence, and it was contagious.

On March 26, 1907, the following was printed in the Bourbon News:

President Clarence LeBus, of the Burley Tobacco Growers' Association, offers to bet $1,000 that the association will win its fight with the trust, and predicts that there will be no burley planted in 1908 if the trust refuses to buy the 1906 and 1907 crops.[14] (Sic)

This offer of wager was extraordinary on several fronts. It certainly was a clear message to his partners in the pool that he was extremely confident of success, and that they should be as well. Secondly, the 1907 crop was not even in the ground yet, but he was clearly demonstrating that he already has plans for that planting and, of all things, the 1908 crop as well. Thirdly, it can be seen as a clear message to James Duke that the pool wasn't going anywhere: He was told precisely what to expect, and the implication was, of course, that there was really nothing he could do about it. (It should also be noted that the $1,000 figure in 1907 equates to about $20,000 by today's values, and that it could have been seen as a direct challenge to Duke: He was one of the few people involved who had that much. Of course the news of the offer to wager spread throughout the region. It was a statement of extreme confidence, and it was meant to put the people at ease and James Duke on notice.

A second and well timed strategy of the pool leadership was an event planned and held at Woodland Park in Lexington. All members of the BTS/pool were invited to attend a picnic to be held on April 26, 1907. The intent of the affair was to instill confidence in the poolers and to enhance the feeling of solidarity.

The picnic ended up being an absolute extravaganza. There were one hundred and eleven men listed on the reception committee alone. Fully fifty men were on the barbecue committee. Forty hogs and forty sheep were barbecued. Twenty-five hundred gallons of burgoo were served to the visitors on 21,000 plates. Special trains brought people from all over Kentucky. The parade passed from downtown, through the High Street neighborhoods, and then to the park. Six thousand people marched in the parade. Podiums were set up in three different locations in the park for multiple dignitaries to speak. Two other overflow stands were set up and supervised by Clarence LeBus. The event was huge! The people left with the conviction that they were all in it together and that there was no way they were going to ever again tolerate seven cent tobacco.[15]

Not only did Clarence LeBus and the leadership manage

to keep the BTS/pool membership intact, engaged, and positive, but they actually managed to inspire an increase in participation. April of 1907 saw the membership increase to a staggering eighty-four percent of all the Kentucky burley growers. This was the time of the height of optimism in the movement.

In May of 1907, the burley tobacco farmers began to set out their crops for the summer growing season. The weather in the summer of 1906 had not been ideal, and it showed in the finished products. The pooled tobacco was somewhat inferior to most previous crops. The Kentucky farmers were, of course, hoping for better weather during 1907, and they went about the process of setting and cultivating their crops as if there had been no 1906. It was what they knew how to do, what they had always done; and it's what they did once more. The burley farmers were operating from a position of hopefulness, and that feeling showed no signs of waning.

* * *

The crop of 1907 was, in fact, very good. Once again, the farmers were advanced the 5 cents for every pound that they sent to the pool. There was hope that James Duke would recognize the superior quality of the 1907 crop and see a way to buy the pooled tobacco, but he continued to thumb his nose at the BTS/pool and its members. By late 1907, the ATC/trust had not bought a single pound of either the 1906 or the 1907 crops. Even in the face of this, the farmers in the pool remained mostly positive with regards to the ultimate outcome.

The topics of discussion throughout Kentucky revolved around one question, and that was how much burley did James Duke have left. It was no secret that he had to have burley for cigarette production, but everything in his actions sent the message that he had an unlimited supply. Was he getting it somewhere else? Had he figured out how to make cigarettes without the white burley? Or was he just bluffing? The answers would dictate the outcomes of the pooling effort.

> *From The Louisville Times, Louisville, KY, Nov. 30, 1907*
>
> What effect this threat (the-cut out effort) will have depends largely on the deep, dark secret of the trust which every official guards as closely as his life, and that is – what is the amount of tobacco the trust has on hand.
>
> This is the great question and the problem: How much leaf tobacco has the trust on hand? 16 (sic)

Clarence LeBus continued pushing his position that ultimately Duke must have the burley. His every word and action sent a signal that he knew something that no one else knew. He acted like he knew exactly how much white burley Duke had in his possession. LeBus's message was clear: "We will win!" And it was remarkable the degree to which the people around him trusted and believed in him. In almost every newspaper throughout the region short articles announced that no tobacco would be grown in that particular county.

The possibility of a "cutout" where the growers would not grow any burley was discussed from the onset of the pool, but it was in late 1907 that the issue was raised in earnest. The entire 1906 and 1907 crops had gone unsold and Clarence LeBus determined that for the pool to be successful, there could be no more burley tobacco grown anywhere. The idea of a strike in the agricultural world was revolutionary. A cutout represented a wholesale transformation of the relationship between industrialism and agriculture. When James Duke announced that he had another source of burley, Clarence LeBus sensed a bluff and announced that the BTS/ pool membership would plant no tobacco crop in 1908. James Duke veered, and on January 3, 1908 he sent his Vice President, R. K. Smith, to Winchester to view samples and make an offer of twelve cents per pound for all of the pooled tobacco. That was almost double what the farmers received in 1905, but LeBus didn't hesitate in turning down the offer. He reminded the members that the heart of the pooling plan was that the demand price was then fifteen cents per pound.

During the heat of the clamor, an emissary of James Duke offered to pay Clarence LeBus $250,000 for the tobacco that LeBus still held if he would sell the pooled crops from both years to The American Tobacco Company for a price that is to this day still unknown. The price was most likely the twelve cents per pound that had just been rejected in Winchester. What was known was that Clarence LeBus immediately rejected the offer that he determined to be a bribe cleverly disguised as well as ingenuity could devise. When asked if the bribe angered him he just laughed.[17]

There would be no burley planted in the summer of 1908. Once again the BTS/pool membership came on board, but it was not without hesitation. Certainly there was a lot of speculation and discussion concerning the wisdom of LeBus's refusal to take the offered twelve cents per pound. The Executive Committee of the BTS/pool was anxious for something to happen. Since two pooled crops remained unsold, it would be virtually impossible to finance another crop. The twelve cents seemed huge, but Clarence LeBus had clearly demonstrated the extent of his wisdom and negotiating skills. He presented the cutout initiative as a "knockout blow." Slowly some tobacco could be sold to the independents, and the overall supply would dwindle. His message to James Duke was clear: There would be no more tobacco. He could either take what was pooled or do without burley altogether.

The prospects of the strike's achieving success were also naturally viewed skeptically by many outside observers. Encouraging hard-pressed farmers to deny planting the region's cash crop seemed an impossible chore. Labor strikes before 1908 succeeded mainly in demonstrating the futility of such activities. For the strike to be successful, nearly all of the 121,000 acres of burley had to be eliminated, and, of course, those who chose to plant the crop could expect to receive huge prices from the ATC/trust buyers in the fall. Ultimately only 16,250 acres were planted by the non-poolers. About 115,000 acres that were normally planted in burley tobacco were cut out. Over 30,000 Kentucky farmers joined the effort and supported Clarence LeBus in his decision. It was a huge show of solidarity.

Two weeks after the rejection of the twelve cent offer, Clarence LeBus met with Kentucky governor Augustus Willson in preparation for a conference to be held in New York between James Duke and LeBus. The intent of the meeting was to break the stalemate, but there was no price agreement: James Duke wouldn't budge. The only thing that came from the meeting was the reinforcement of LeBus's belief that, since Duke was eager for the meeting, he was getting nervous about his supply.

In short order, on March 11, 1908, the first sale was made to The ATC/trust since the fight began. The sale was consummated in Winchester, Kentucky. One thousand hogsheads (1,200,000 pounds) of the 1906 burley sold for fifteen cents per pound. This was a significant increase over the twelve cents offer made for all of the pooled tobacco made six weeks earlier. This sale was for some of the inferior 1906 crop and was perceived by some to be a sure sign that the struggle was over. Clarence LeBus believed that it was a sign that James Duke was beginning to panic.

Rumors began to fly that the war was over. Newspapers were announcing the end of the struggle. The Society of Equity made an official statement that the ATC/trust had agreed to pay sixteen and eighteen cents for the 1906-07 crops. What they failed to say was that Clarence LeBus didn't accept that offer. LeBus and the BTS/pool denied there was any agreement.

It was in the spring months of March, April and May of 1908 that the movement was increasingly the subject of doubt and ridicule by men who were not members of the BTS/pool but were mostly elected officials. To these politicians it was seen as politically expedient to question the decisions of LeBus and the BTS/pool leadership. Ultimately the governor himself insinuated in a speech that BTS/pool and its leaders were in collusion with the American Tobacco Company to enable the trust to more effectively control the tobacco marketing.

To top it off, Governor Augustus Willson made direct charges that the BTS/pool was dominated by shrewd managers who were ambitious to increase the power that had come to them. Without doubt, the charges were directed at Clarence LeBus. His confidence and reluctance to sell the tobacco at a price that seemed to some to be very high , but was lower than he thought they could ultimately get, was confusing to some. If the members of the pool were becoming frustrated they did not show it in the response to Willson's accusations: There was universal condemnation of the governor, and the pool members were earnest and zealous in their support of the BTS/pool and Clarence LeBus. It was noted that the only tobacco sold to the trust was at Willson's suggestion.[18]

The celebrated activist, writer and educator, Ms. Alice Lloyd, was an ardent supporter of the BTS/pool. She was known for her fearless presentation when taking a position, and she clearly demonstrated just that in her speech at a BTS/pool meeting in Louisville.

> *The Daily Public Ledger, Maysville, Kentucky, March 31, 1908:*
>
> Spotlight Turned on Miss Alice Lloyd
>
> Something About the Woman Who is Today the Idol of Kentucky's Tobacco Growers.
>
> Senator elect W.O.Bradley, Govenor Augustus E. Willson, J.B.Duke, Clarence LeBus, and President Roosevelt himself are in total eclipse in Louisville today.
>
> The spotlight has been removed from the men. Today in Louisville, someone else is in the spotlight and she is getting all of the attention. She dresses in black, with a sparkling blue eye that can look daggers when the occasion demands it, and with a brilliant mind, and a keen tongue that knows where and when to do the most effective lashing. She has a soft sweet voice and culture and refinement are apparent in every utterance and movement. She is the Joan of Arc of the Burley tobacco growers. Miss Alice Lloyd is the spokesman of 40,000 of the best men on earth, men who wear brown jeans, but are

the equal of any man at the rostrum or in the audience at the Burley Tobacco Society's law and order meeting yesterday.

Miss Lloyd was seen this morning and asked if she came to Louisville to make a speech and goad the Governor into replying.

"Certainly not," she said this morning. "I simply came down to hear and see, but at the same time, I determined that if any misstatements were made about the tobacco growers, I would correct them. That was all. I simply couldn't help doing that.

Oh, if the people only knew the truth. If they only knew the struggle of the men in the Burley District. If they only knew how brave, how loyal, and how patient these men have been. And they are real Kentuckians. They are the men who have made the State and it makes me furious to think of any of our own blood and bone siding against our own men, women and children with a foreign corporation, grasping at everything in sight. That is why I talked. I was so excited. I know I did not do our cause justice. Oh, if I could have just said something that would have fired the heart of every farmer in Kentucky. But I never cease to hope and pray that we will win, and we will. If I just made one point or if I put one person to thinking at the meeting yesterday, I shall be happier over that than anything I ever did in my life." (Sic)

"GOVERNOR GOT MAD."

"But my goodness didn't the Governor get mad? I was so sorry too, but I had to tell him what the people think. He was real cold after the meeting, but I just can't help it. Oh, I shall be so happy if I think the society men think I did something useful or helpful to them, but so broken up if I made even one mistake." (Sic)

Miss Lloyd is perhaps 35 years old. Her home is near Dover and she was once the head of a girl's school at Richmond, and

> recently volunteered her services to write a series of articles for the American Society of Equity. Many of her articles have appeared in publications in the Bluegrass. She left Louisville this morning for Winchester, the headquarters of the Burley Tobacco Society.[19]

The summer of 1908 was, for the most part, uneventful. Overtures by both sides were nothing more that routine repetition of the same old words: an offer to buy at fifteen cents followed by rejection. Clarence LeBus surveyed the fields and determined that, assuredly, very little burley had been set out. James Duke's agents surveyed the same fields and determined exactly the same thing. To LeBus the absence of tobacco in the fields was a significant sign, and his confidence was reinforced. For James Duke it started to sink in that the tobacco already pooled was all there would be. Still there was no settlement. Both sides dug in.

The negotiations stalled. The 1908 strike had reached an impasse: eventually the financial pressure would become so great that one side or the other would have to yield. Either the American Tobacco Company would need the pooled tobacco for its own financial survival, or the BTS/pool members could not endure the continued hardships of the prolonged strike.

The coming of autumn brought Clarence LeBus some significant criticism. Summer was over, and the almost vacation-like ease created by having no crop to raise was over. The farmers began to face the reality that there would be no money coming their way that year. They began to wonder what was wrong with LeBus. The pool had chance after chance to sell the burley for fifteen cents, but their leader dug in and refused to even consider that price. The rumbling intensified as the fall slipped into late October and early November. Those closest to Clarence LeBus continued to support his approach. The county leadership of the BTS/pool continued to articulate confidence, but many were beginning to question, in private, the wisdom of not selling. Every signal cast by James Duke displayed a lack of concern.

Duke's signals of nonchalance was met by LeBus's continued display of confidence. Clarence LeBus's message did not change from early spring of 1908, through that summer, nor into late fall of the same year.

> *From The Bourbon News, Paris, KY, April 07, 1908 (Quoting LeBus)*
>
> Even if there should be a crop in 1909 the leaf could not be marketed until 1910.
>
> "The 160,000,000 pounds of white Burley now in the pool must be the supply of the world for two years. Some months ago when we said 1906 Burley would sell for fifteen cents a pound, some people laughed. It is now selling for that figure, but we have not fixed a price for the 1907 leaf, and will not do so yet. Manufactures of tobacco must have it, and they must pay for it.[20] (Sic)

The Pressure mounted, and LeBus's support started to show signs of cracking. In some circles he became the butt of ridicule. The questions being asked by increasingly more and more grass-roots farmers were casting doubt on his leadership and his honesty. They began to suggest again that he was in cahoots with Duke. They thought his refusal to sell was putting the entire pooling effort in jeopardy. They said he didn't understand the needs of the small farmers. When he would hear of the criticism, Clarence Lebus's reaction was always the same: He would smile or laugh.[21] What the man did not do, was budge.

The stalemate finally ended in November of 1908, when Clarence LeBus played what the Cincinnati Enquirer called, "the great bluff." LeBus had received offers of purchase of small quantities of the pooled burley from small independent producers, and he cleverly leaked news of this to the press. He quoted amounts purchased that were greatly exaggerated. Later he was heard taunting an American Tobacco Company agent, saying that the BTS/pool no longer "cared a farthing" whether the ATC/trust purchased a single pound. He said that the independent producers would buy every pound that the BTS/pool had pooled and would buy it at the BTS/pool price. The bluff worked. Fearing that large amounts, or perhaps all, of the pooled leaf might be sold, James Duke and his American Tobacco Company caved. They began to negotiate with the BTS/pool in earnest.[22]

On November 17, 1908, Clarence LeBus and nineteen other men representing the BTS/pool checked into the Brown-Procteria Hotel in Louisville. What the men did know was that they would be negotiating with the American Tobacco Company over the sale of the pooled tobacco. What they didn't know was that the meeting would last for three days and nights.

The talks had barely begun in the evening of the seventeenth when the first sticking point came fast and furious. The BTS/pool had insisted from the first that twenty-five percent of the total pounds sold would be offered to the independent buyers and manufacturers at whatever price was agreed upon. Of course this was rejected by the ATC/trust. James Duke did not want his competitors to have any of the pooled crops. The ATC/trust representatives said they would buy no tobacco if the independents were in on the sale. Clarence LeBus replied that the meetings were over: no sales to independents, no sales at all. The ATC/trust changed their minds rather quickly, and the talks resumed. Independents were to buy twenty-five percent.

The negotiations commenced the next morning. Ultimately, after hours of wrangling, the American Tobacco Company agreed to buy the entire remaining 1906 crop at twenty and one half cents per pound and three fourths of the 1907 crop at sixteen cents per pound (Most of the 1906 crop that remained was of the higher grades, the lower grades having been sold over time to independents). The BTS/pool members present were jubilant: The price agreed upon was more than most would have imagined a few weeks earlier. But their joy was short-lived: LeBus quickly rejected the offer. He succinctly stated that the price for the 1907 crop was seventeen cents a pound and nothing less.

The talks stalled, and those around LeBus begged him to agree to the sixteen cent offer. They did everything they could to convince him that the ATC/trust would pull out altogether if they didn't settle. Every other member of the board was ready to mob him, but he wouldn't budge.

Ultimately the ATC/trust came back to the table with another offer: They raised the offer on the 1907 crop to sixteen and one half cents per pound. Again Clarence LeBus refused, and again his board members went crazy with indignation. Ultimately he convinced his board that James Duke would agree to the seventeen cent price. As a group, they wanted to vote against LeBus and accept the sixteen and one half cent offer, but his control was just too great for the men as individuals to go against him.

On November 20, 1908 at 4:05 pm, after three days of grueling non-stop conflict, it was announced that The American Tobacco Company agreed to pay about $12,000,000 for the tobacco pooled by the BTS/pool. The average price paid for the 1906 crop (12,000,000 pounds) was twenty and one half cents per pound. The 63,000,000 pounds of 1907 tobacco sold for seventeen cents!

Clarence LeBus wasn't finished. He demanded that the ATC/trust pay an additional three dollars per hogshead in "outage fees." These were the fees for packing and storing the tobacco in warehouse. The ATC/trust at first refused, but because of fear that the entire deal might fall apart, they ultimately agreed to pay what totaled $250,000.

Cincinnati Commercial Tribune, Cincinnati, Ohio, November 7, 1909

When the trust paid $17 (per hundred) for the tobacco in the pool, it was not because it wanted to and not because the governing board of the Burley society would not have accepted $2 less: $17 was LeBus' price.[23] (Sic)

When the news of the Louisville success passed, the celebrations were huge and spontaneous. Grown men laughed and danced like young boys. The financial implications were huge after years of no tobacco income. Bourbon County received approximately $750,000; Woodford County about $500,000; Scott County approximately $900,000; and Bracken County, almost $100,000.[24]

Clarence LeBus became a celebrated star in Kentucky. "LeBus for Governor" signs appeared everywhere. He was considered to be somewhat of a folk hero and an undisputed champion of the little man. Everyone benefitted from LeBus's leadership: the little man, the wealthy land-owners, and, of course, Clarence LeBus himself.

Certainly Clarence LeBus's accomplishments were astonishing with the solidarity/pooling effort. His abilities go unquestioned, but as one contemporary said, "We all know about his math skills, but the biggest sum he ever done was making seven cents equal seventeen."

Burley Tobacco on the LeBus Warehouse floor.

AN IRON-WILLED GIANT

Program for the Hinata Horserace Event

CHAPTER TEN

Twenty years after the celebrated "cut-out," Clarence LeBus died at his Cynthiana home. He died at eleven PM on Monday night, June 18, 1928. He had been ill for only a few days. The cause of death was diabetes and heart trouble. At his bedside were his wife and two sons when he passed. He was sixty-six.

His death closed the book on one of the most remarkable chapters in Kentucky history and ended the astonishing career of one of its most notable citizens.

Mr. LeBus continued his efforts to administer the Burley Tobacco Society after the success of the 1906-1908 pooling efforts, but it became an uphill battle. Dealing with people from within the organization became as difficult as it had been dealing with James Duke. Clarence LeBus certainly benefited as a result of the movement: His financial gain was huge, and that became an issue. The payment of his $25,000 salary came right off the top of the receipts from the settlement sales, and there was also the huge profits he made from the sale of his own tobacco as well. It's not surprising that jealously eventually entered into the equation: It usually does when one has more than the other.

When the discussions concerning the status of the BTS/pool going forward commenced, Clarence LeBus and the BTS/pool leadership proposed a ten percent fee that every member would have to pay when joining the new BTS/pool. The fee was to be used for expenses and to build a manufacturing plant that would make cigarettes with the goal of eventually bypassing the American Tobacco Company entirely. There was an immediate and negative reaction to this proposal. Unfounded charges regarding LeBus and his previous benefits began to fly around. When politicians entered the fray, the BTS/pool began what would be a slow death.

The Burley Tobacco Society was not organized with democratic features, and that, combined with the proposed ten percent charge, eventually alienated farmers, especially small holders and tenants. There were no changes in the organizational structure, and the subsequent cooperative attempts fell prey to dissension. By 1910 it had become obvious that farmers no longer viewed the tobacco cooperative as a vehicle of salvation. A rapid collapse followed. With remarkable suddenness, the subject of most burley farmers' criticisms became not the ATC/trust, but rather the leadership of the BTS/pool and chiefly, its president, Clarence LeBus.[1]

Those closest to Clarence LeBus in the BTS Leadership were quite sure of his honesty and of his personal integrity. They believed, without doubt, that his primary concern was always with the farmers, and that he was committed to the Burley Tobacco Society members and not to his own personal gain. It is important to note that before Clarence LeBus joined the BTS/pool, he had immense business and farm holdings. When he took on the responsibility of president of the BTS/pool, he hired a manager to run his farms and other businesses. His $25,000 salary was contingent upon the success of the pool: He knew that if he failed to outmaneuver James Duke, he would be paid nothing. Early in 1908 when the ATC/trust offered twelve cents and then fifteen cents, LeBus could have closed the deal, collected his $25,000 and gone home. But he didn't. It's also revealing that during the two years of the initial pooling effort, Clarence LeBus paid all of his own expenses for travel, lodging, meals, and everything else.

LeBus returned to his life of running his own businesses and farms, but, for almost five years, he kept working part time in an effort to keep the pool alive. It was a hopeless endeavor. When he left the organization for good, he refused to join all subsequent pooling attempts, and in fact, he competed with the future pooling efforts through his own warehouses. The movement died.

The success and conclusion of the BTS/pool didn't slow down Mr. LeBus. He continued his efforts of buying and owning more farmland, and he remained engaged in the banking business. He entered into a multitude of other business ventures as well. His farms continued their profitable trends, and his other businesses were mostly profitable. He shifted his interest to bigger and better farms in Fayette and Bourbon counties. On October 12, 1912, he bought the magnificent 465 acre Lane Farm on the corner of the Ironworks Pike and Russell Cave Road (across the road from the Jot-Em-Down Store) just north of Lexington. Soon his wife decided to change the name to Hinata Farm, and the couple decided to make it their home.

When Clarence's wife Mary made the move, Lexington became her new home in every way. She enjoyed the social life, and in short order she reached the pinnacle of Blue Grass society. Rarely a day passed that her name wasn't to be found in one of the local newspapers. Her crowning social triumph was a private thoroughbred race meet held at her Hinata Farm. The extravaganza was held on April 24, 1913, and everybody who was deemed important was invited. It was (and still is) the only race, not held at a regular track, ever sanctioned by the Kentucky State Racing Commission. There were four races, first rate horses, and professional jockeys. The list of Judges and Stewards was like a Who's Who in Kentucky. A grandstand was erected, huge tents were set up, and a luncheon was served. Early in the day, cars and carriages were lined from Lexington to Hinata. It was a grand social event.

Clarence LeBus did initially make Hinata his home, and he, in fact, moved there; but it didn't take long before he was spending much more time back at his Cynthiana home than he was in Lexington. His office, his warehouse, and most of his farms were in Harrison County, and it was there that he stayed. Cynthiana was his home: Hinata was a place he visited and occasionally stayed.

Clarence LeBus showed no signs whatsoever of slowing down. His disengagement from the BTS/pool gave him the time to do what he had always done best: buy and sell tobacco, and buy more farmland. That is exactly what he did.

Clarence LeBus eventually owned every large river bottom farm that bordered Cynthiana. His farms included the famous A-Keller farm (at the end of A-Keller Lane) that he inherited from his father. The magnificent Howk's Farm (where the Waste Water Treatment plant now sits), the Lake Farm (on US 27 North, bordering the bypass), The Handy Farm (Flat Run Veterans Park), the Abdellah Park Farm (Laddish/Easy Pack factories), and the Handy/Desha bottoms (the Walmart development area). He was a huge producer of cattle, sheep, horses, and hogs as well as tobacco.

Ultimately Clarence LeBus was a director and part owner of ten banks, two in Cincinnati, two in Indiana, five in Kentucky, and one in St. Louis. He was president of The Cincinnati Iron Fence Company, and in Cynthiana he owned The Clarence LeBus and Sons tobacco Company, the Cynthiana Livestock Sales, the Bluegrass Garage, a pork processing company, a service station, and a restaurant.

After his purchase of the Hinata farm, Clarence LeBus concentrated his land buying to some of the best farms around Lexington. He started with land that joined his Hinata farm, and it grew from there. Ultimately he owned land continuously from the Russell Cave Road to Paris Pike. Two properties with well-known names that he owned were The Claiborne Stock Farm and the famous Escondida Farm.

When Clarence LeBus died his land holdings amounted to a staggering 37,000 acres.

The tales and stories of Clarence LeBus still float around Cynthiana today. Ask any Cynthiana native over fifty years old if they have heard of the man, and they will probably recall a story that was told to them by their fathers or grandfathers. These recollections are always positive and usually funny. It's been over one hundred years since his heyday, so of course the stories have been passed down, told and retold thousands of times. As is always the case, a lot gets lost through the repeated tellings. The truths of what actually happened so long ago have been overgrown by the weeds of fable. What is startling, though, is that, after so much time, Clarence LeBus still lives in this local lore.

Clarence LeBus opens 2 banks in one day!

MARK MATTMILLER

MARK MATTMILLER

www.ingramcontent.com/pod-product-compliance
Lightning Source LLC
Chambersburg PA
CBHW071002080526
44587CB00015B/2317